W9-CEY-529

We usually think of CAPTAIN JAMES COOK as the man who discovered Australia and New Zealand, but he was much more than just an intrepid explorer. He was also a scientist whose flair for mathematics and skilful use of the latest scientific equipment revolutionized accurate chart-making. Although there still exist mariner's guides from more than two thousand years ago, it was Cook's detailed survey of the Newfoundland coasts and his three great voyages of exploration in the Pacific that laid the foundation for modern scientific navigation and charting of the waters of the Earth.

Cook's first voyage, in the *Endeavour*, marked the beginning of the great age of scientific exploration when, in 1768, he set off round the world with a party of scientists to plot the course of the planet Venus. The plant life gathered, illustrated and described on the way was to form a botanical collection whose like had never before been seen in Europe.

Dr. Williams follows the adventures and achievements of this remarkable man, carefully explaining all the technical terms introduced. The book contains more than fifty illustrations, a date chart, reading list and index.

Dr. TREVOR I. WILLIAMS has been editor of the international scientific review *Endeavour* since 1954, and has long had an active interest in the history of science and technology. Apart from purely scientific works, he was a joint editor of *A History of Technology* (1954–58); wrote, with T. K. Derry, *A Short History of Technology* (1960); and edited *A Biographical Dictionary of Scientists* (1968).

He has also written *Alfred Nobel, Pioneer of High Explosives* for the *Pioneers of Science and Discovery* series.

Captain James Cook, R.N. (1728–79)
by John Webber, R.A.

James Cook
Scientist and Explorer

Trevor I. Williams

Wayland

Other Books in this Series

Carl Benz and the Motor Car   Doug Nye

George Eastman and the Early Photographers   Brian Coe

Richard Arkwright and Cotton Spinning   Richard L. Hills

James Simpson and Chloroform   R. S. Atkinson

Edward Jenner and Vaccination   A. J. Harding Rains

Louis Pasteur and Microbiology   H. I. Winner

Alfred Nobel, Pioneer of High Explosives   Trevor I. Williams

Michael Faraday and Electricity   Brian Bowers

Ernest Rutherford and the Atom   P. B. Moon

Rudolf Diesel and the Diesel Engine   John F. Moon

Thomas Telford, Father of Civil Engineering   Keith Ellis

Isaac Newton and Gravity   P. M. Rattansi

Thomas Edison, Genius of Electricity   Keith Ellis

Alexander Fleming and Penicillin   W. Howard Hughes

Marie Stopes and Birth Control   H. V. Stopes-Roe and Ian Scott

William Harvey and Blood Circulation   Eric Neil

Joseph Lister and Antisepsis   William Merrington

Gregor Mendel and Heredity   Wilma George

Alexander Graham Bell and the Telephone   Andrew McElroy

Charles Darwin and Evolution   D. R. Brothwell

SBN 85078 191 4
Copyright © by Trevor I. Williams
First published in 1974 by
Wayland Publishers Limited
49 Lansdowne Place, Hove, East Sussex BN3 1HF
Second impression 1980
Printed and bound in Great Britain
at The Pitman Press, Bath

Contents

List of Illustrations 6

1 Early Problems of Navigation and the Exploration of the Pacific 9

2 Cook's Early Life 34

3 The *Endeavour* Voyage 41

4 The Achievements of the *Endeavour* Voyage 57

5 The Voyage of *Resolution* and *Adventure* 63

6 The Fatal Third Voyage: *Resolution* and *Discovery* 73

7 The Man and his Achievement 83

Date Chart 89

Glossary 91

Reading List 93

Index 94

Illustrations

Captain Cook (by Webber)	*frontispiece*
Captain Cook (after Dance)	8
Ferdinand Magellan	10
Vasco de Balboa	10
Ptolemy's world map	12
Abraham Ortelius	13
Ortelius's New World Map	13
The *Victoria*	14
Chart of Pitcairn Island	15
The old Royal Observatory, Greenwich	16
Quadrant	16
Astrolabe	17
Astrolabe in use	17
Cross-staff	18
Davis's back-staff	19
Harrison's Timekeeper No. 4	19
Ship's wooden log	20
Gerard Mercator	21
Mercator's map of the southern hemisphere	21
Hernando Cortes in Mexico	22
16th/17th c. voyages of Pacific discovery	24
18th c. voyages of Pacific discovery	25
The *Golden Hind*	26
Sir Francis Drake	26
Drake's dial	26
Abel Tasman's encounter with Maoris	28
John Byron's meeting with Pacific islanders	30
Samuel Wallis's meeting with Oberea	30
Louis Antoine de Bougainville	32
Hadley's octant	32
Sextant	33
Title page, *Nautical Almanac*	33
James Cook's birthplace	34
Captain Hugh Palliser	35
"The Press Gang"—1770 cartoon	36
Venus in transit in 1874	38
Venus in transit from two points of observation	38
Alexander Dalrymple	39
The Royal Society's house, Crane Court	39
The *Endeavour*	40
The Teredo worm	41
Sir Joseph Banks	42
Daniel Solander	42

Plan of Success Bay, Tierra del Fuego 44–45
Cook's chart of Tierra del Fuego 45
Cook's plan of Tahiti 46
View of Tahiti 47
Maori war canoe, New Zealand 48–49
The Perforated Rock, Tolago Bay, New Zealand 50
Cook's chart of New Zealand 51
A Maori hippah, New Zealand 52–53
The *Endeavour* being repaired in New Holland 54–55
Portable observatory housing Shelton's pendulum clock 56–57
Extract, *Nautical Almanac* 59
Title page, *Beginnings of a Flora of New Zealand* 61
Sir Joseph Banks 61
Kangaroo 62
The Forsters 64
Cook in the Ice Islands 64–65
A white bear 66
Bread fruit 67
Tools of Tahiti 67
The *Resolution* and *Adventure* in Tahiti 68
Easter Island 69
James Burney discovers the massacre of a party of the
   Adventure's men in New Zealand 70
James Cook (by Josiah Wedgwood) 72
Omai 72–73
Kerguelen's Island 74
Family of Van Diemen's Land 75
Canoe of the Sandwich Islands 76
Cook and his officers being entertained on one of the
   Sandwich Islands 76
House interior, Nootka Sound 77
Sea lions shot for fresh provisions 78
Cook's friendly welcome in Hawaii 79
Cook's death in Hawaii 80–81
The *Discovery* and the *Resolution* in Kamchatka 82
Ceremonial dance of Tahiti 84–85
Detail of Dance's portrait of Cook 86

1 *Early Problems of Navigation and the Exploration of the Pacific*

By any standard, James Cook was a remarkable man. Of humble origin—his father was a farm labourer—he had little formal education, and none at all after the age of twelve. As a young man he enlisted as an ordinary seaman in the Navy, and rose to become an officer whose name ranks with those of Drake and Nelson. He combined with practical seamanship a flair for mathematics and the use of scientific instruments which enabled him to bring to chart-making a revolutionary degree of precision. His scientific work earned him the coveted distinction of Fellowship of the Royal Society. He transformed our knowledge of the geography of the Pacific; such was his accuracy in surveying that even today—two centuries later—a British Admiralty chart for Pickersgill Harbour in New Zealand is described as "from Captain Cook's voyage of 1773." Over and above all this, he was a man of outstanding courage and determination, able to inspire confidence in his men on long voyages involving great hardship and peril.

To this last aspect we will return later, when we follow Cook's three great Pacific voyages, first in *Endeavour* (1766–71), then in *Discovery* and *Adventure* (1772–75), and finally in *Discovery* and *Resolution* (1776–80), which led to his lonely, tragic death at the far ends of the earth. The exploration of space today is akin to the exploration of the remoter parts of the earth as little as two centuries ago—that is, within the lifetime of the grandparents of some people alive today. In the last analysis, today's astronauts must face the possibility that despite the immense technical resources that support them some mishap may still put them beyond rescue. This, too, was the lot of

Captain Cook—an engraving taken from the painting by Sir Nathaniel Dance (1734–1811). Dance was appointed, in 1768, one of the foundation members of the Royal Academy.

explorers in Cook's time, and, indeed, until much later. Once they sailed into uncharted seas their very whereabouts were unknown; no one could rescue them. Only their own resources, and resourcefulness, could bring them safe home again. James Cook himself had the narrowest of escapes when *Endeavour* ran aground on the Great Barrier Reef of Australia. Not until the beginning of this century, with the discovery of wireless telegraphy, did the situation radically change.

No assessment of Cook and his work is possible without some knowledge of the charting of the Pacific already made by earlier explorers, and of the navigational aids available to him. The first European ever to set eyes on the Pacific Ocean was Vasco de Balboa (1475–1517) in 1513, from a mountain peak on the Isthmus of Darien, the narrow strip of land that joins North and South America, and separates the Atlantic from the Pacific. Balboa was quite literally the first, for he had deliberately left his followers a little way behind. He waded down into the sea and

Above left Ferdinand Magellan (c. 1480–1521), the Portuguese navigator whose expedition, mounted in 1519, made the first circumnavigation of the world.

Above right Vasco Nunez de Balboa (1475–1517), the Spanish explorer. In 1510, to escape creditors, he joined Francisco de Enisco's expedition to Darien—as a stowaway. In 1513 he set out to cross the Isthmus of Panama and became the first European to see the Pacific Ocean.

claimed it, and all the regions upon whose shores it beat, in the name of the crown of Castile and Leon. The event was historic, and fraught with historic consequences, for it was to add immensely to the wealth and power of Spain and lead to bitter rivalry with other European powers. Tragically, Balboa's reward was to be beheaded four years later, on the ground that he was seeking to become too powerful.

Balboa's gift to his sovereign was enormous, for the Pacific is some 10,000 miles wide at the equator and extends north and south almost as far; in all, it covers some 70 million square miles. It is a lonely ocean, on which one can be nearly 2,000 miles from the nearest land, and that perhaps only a small island.

The first to sail upon this vast uncharted expanse—greater in area than all the earth's dry land—was the famous Portuguese navigator, Ferdinand Magellan (c. 1480–1521). He entered it six years later in 1519 through the stormy strait, at the tip of South America, which bears his name. His object was mainly commercial. The unreliable world maps of his day, and an underestimate of the length of a degree of longitude, made him believe that if he could reach the Moluccas, by way of the Pacific, he could prove that these rich spice islands lay in the half of the world containing new territories that the arbitrary Papal Bull of 1493 had allocated to Spain, not Portugal. A year later the dividing line in the western hemisphere had been drawn 370 leagues west of the Cape Verde Islands. And so it mattered where the dividing line—180 degrees of longitude away—lay in the eastern hemisphere.

The sighting of the Pacific did not itself show what land it might enclose. Nor did it prove that there was another approach to the far eastern lands that had already been reached from the west. For all men knew, there might be another great land barrier stretching north and south as impenetrably as the Americas.

That the earth was spherical had long been recognized by learned men. As early as the third century B.C. the Alexandrian scholar Eratosthenes had not merely asserted this, but had measured the size of the earth with surprising accuracy; his estimate is not far from the truth. But how land and sea covered the globe outside the ancient world was quite unknown. Ignorance, however, did not stop speculation, and speculation—if general enough—can become confused with truth. Thus Pomponius Mela, in the first century A.D., declared that the southern hemisphere was largely oceanic. A century later, Ptolemy claimed that it held a vast unknown continent, and that the Indian Ocean was a landlocked sea. With scarcely a shred of evidence to guide them, men clung fiercely to

Above A late fifteenth century version of a world map based on the writings of Claudius Ptolemy (c. 90–c. 168 A.D.), an Egyptian astronomer, mathematician and geographer. His idea that Asia extended far further east than it really does gave strength to the idea that it would be quickly reached by travelling westward.

such views. Thus in 1570 the great Flemish geographer Ortelius (1527–98) published a world map showing a vast *Terra Australis nondum cognita* (southern land not yet discovered). People felt there must be a great land mass in the south to balance Europe and Asia in the north, but nobody ever actually explained why. About the only tangible evidence was offered by the great Venetian traveller Marco Polo (1254–1324), who with his father and uncle arrived at the court of Kubla Khan in 1275 in China, from where he made some remarkable journeys in Asia, not returning to Venice until 1295. His account of his travels seemed to imply the existence of an immensely rich land south of Java, but this was probably Cambodia.

The fact was that at around 1500 there were huge tracts of the world's surface, including the Pacific Ocean, whose nature was quite unknown—as unknown as the back of the moon was to us until a few years ago. The only way to find out what lay there was to go and see, and a few brave seafarers—hoping for gain and fame—were ready to take up the challenge and found backers to support them. In judging their

Below left Abraham Ortelius (1527–1598) of Antwerp, cartographer and dealer in maps, books and antiques. His famous *Theatrum Orbis Terrarum*, published in 1570, was regularly revised in the light of new facts and discoveries. *Below right* The title *cartouche* from the New World Map in Ortelius's *Theatrum* showing the "hitherto undiscovered" southern continent which he intended naming after Magellan.

courage we must, however, remember that educated people believed that the world was round, and so could be circumnavigated provided each ocean ran into another. Sir John Mandeville, who wrote a famous book of travel in the fourteenth century, was quite clear about this: "If a man found passages by ships that would go to search the world, men might go by ship all about the world and above and beneath." It is a myth to think that the early explorers believed in a flat earth, from whose edge they might fall to some terrible doom. They well knew the real hazards—shipwreck, mutiny, scurvy, exhaustion of food and water, hostile natives, and inability to get home because of adverse currents and trade winds. Fear of falling over the edge of the world was not in their minds—except perhaps for some of the more ignorant and superstitious members of their crews.

Ferdinand Magellan set out from Seville on 20th September, 1519, with a fleet of five vessels—the largest of only 120 tons—financed mainly by the young Charles I of Spain (later Charles V, Holy Roman Emperor). For Magellan the voyage was ill-starred. After quelling a serious mutiny he eventually lost his life in the Philippines in a needless battle with natives. But one of his ships—the *Victoria*, of only 85 tons—finally came home to Seville on 8th September, 1522. The first circumnavigation of the world had been made and the Pacific crossed from east to west,

The *Victoria* which, under Elcano, was the only one of Magellan's five ships to return safely to Spain after sailing round the world.

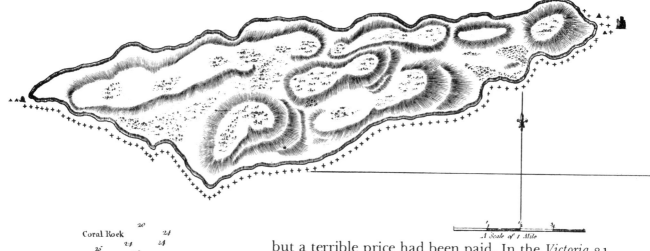

Coral Rock

A Scale of 1 Mile

A chart of Pitcairn Island. This island's position was so miscalculated that Cook's attempt to find it failed. It was rediscovered quite by accident by the mutineers from *H.M.S. Bounty* while fleeing from the British Navy in 1790. Realizing that in this mistake lay their safety, the mutineers landed. The island was not spotted again until 1808. The *Bounty's* captain, William Bligh, had been chosen to be master of the *Resolution* on Cook's second voyage some eighteen years previously.

but a terrible price had been paid. In the *Victoria* 31 men returned, and later four survivors of the *Trinidad* straggled home, but 170 men died in the attempt.

Magellan's voyage was an amazing achievement, the greatest single voyage in history. Ironically, it failed in its immediate objective, for in 1529 Charles V had to acknowledge that the Molucca Islands were within the Portuguese sphere of influence. But it had shown beyond all doubt that whatever land the Pacific might contain it was not a continuous barrier to navigation. It had also showed something of the size of the ocean and to this aspect we must now give some special attention.

Today, with hundreds of satellites orbiting in space, the configuration of the earth is so precisely known that the position of any point on it can be determined within a few feet. This accuracy is fantastic. For example, if one were to ask precisely how far the Houses of Parliament in London are from the Capitol in Washington, we should have to say which part of the Houses of Parliament and which part of the Capitol. In Magellan's day, and for another two centuries, things were very different. On reaching the Philippines one of his navigators—no doubt well versed in the skills of the day—miscalculated its position by more than 52 degrees of longitude. At the latitude of the Philippines a degree of longitude is about 68 miles, so the error was around 3,400 miles. How could such a mistake be made?

A ship's position on the globe is pinpointed by its latitude—indicated by east/west lines on maps—and its longitude—indicated by north/south lines. Latitude is reckoned in degrees from the equator (0°) to the poles (90°); in this case the equator acts as a natural reference line. Longitude has to be expressed in degrees from some predetermined meridian—a great circle running from pole to pole. Any meridian could be chosen, and since 1884 that which runs through Greenwich has been internationally recognized (except by France, which did not fall into line until 1911). Greenwich had been widely used long before that, because it was there that Charles II in 1675 founded his Royal Observatory for "the finding out of the longitude of places for perfecting navigation and astronomy."

Nevertheless, other countries used other meridians. France, for example, used at the instigation of Cardinal Richelieu the meridian of Ferro (one of the Canary Islands) because this lay between the Old and New Worlds, at 20°W. German maps used

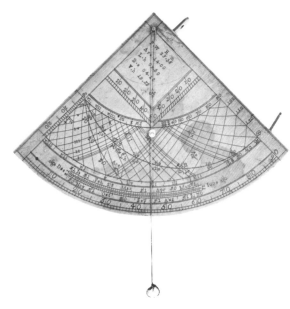

Above One of the first instruments to be used widely at sea for measuring the altitude of stars was the quadrant. This one dates from about 1675. The star is observed through the pinhole sights and its altitude is read off where the plumb-line cuts the scale.

Below Flamsteed House, the old Royal Observatory, Greenwich, was built in 1675 by Charles II for John Flamsteed (1646–1719), the first Astronomer Royal.

the Berlin meridian and Russian that of the Pulkova Observatory. This complicated things for navigators, but presented no real difficulty so long as they remembered to do the right additions or subtractions. Nor, at least in theory, was the actual measurement of latitude very difficult, since one only had accurately to measure the altitude of the sun or a star, such as the Pole Star. At sea, this was not always easy to do. Apart from the motion of small ships in rough seas, cloud or fog might make sightings impossible for days on end.

The instruments for measuring altitude were quite crude: the commonest was the quadrant. As its name implies, it was a quarter-circle of wood or metal, with sights along one edge. The circumference was graduated in degrees from 0° to 90° and a plumb-line was fixed to the angle of the quadrant. When the sights were aligned on the sun or star, the point at which the plumb-line cut the scale measured the altitude. The mariner's astrolabe—a simpler version of the astronomer's astrolabe—was similar in princi-

Above A twelfth century astronomer's astrolabe. The marine version of the astrolabe often had the centre cut away. *Below* Using an astrolabe to measure the angle of altitude of a tower. If the angle is measured in two places and the distance between the two places is known, the height of the tower can be calculated.

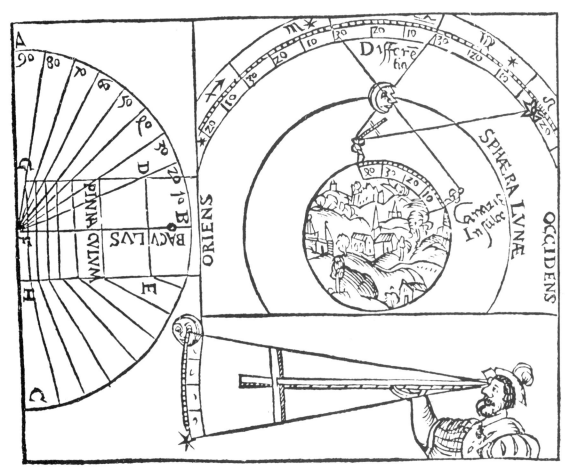

ple. Another simple sighting device was the cross-staff, a wooden rod about three feet long, along which he slid a transverse rod, one end of which was aligned with the horizon and the other with the sun or star. A rather later refinement of this was the back-staff, with two graduated scales, which let the observer turn his back on the sun.

These instruments were not very accurate, partly because of their crude design and partly because of the ship's movement. A lot depended on the skill and experience of the user. Still, it is fair to say that by the sixteenth century mariners were not too much bothered by the problem of latitude. In this respect they knew reasonably well where they were at any given time.

Above A very popular 16th century successor to the astrolabe was the cross-staff. It consisted of a length of wood (about three feet) with a sliding cross piece. This woodcut, published in 1524, shows both its astronomical and its navigational use. A serious disadvantage was that the sun's altitude could be observed only by looking directly at it.

18

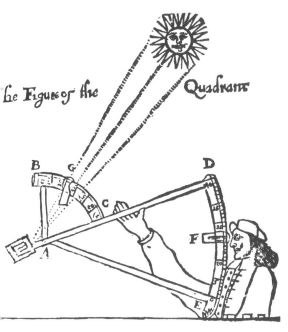

Above A major improvement on the cross-staff was the back-staff, invented by John Davis (c. 1550–1605) in 1594.

Above Timekeeper No. 4, made by John Harrison (1693–1776), which at last solved the problem of the accurate determination of longitude.

The determination of longitude, however, was quite a different problem, and one not really solved until the latter part of the eighteenth century. Measuring longitude depends upon determining the local time relative to a fixed meridian—in practice, the meridian at Greenwich. If the mariner sets off with an accurate clock set to Greenwich time, virtually all he needs to do in order to find out his longitude wherever he may be weeks or months later, is to note the time on the clock at which the sun crosses the meridian. Unfortunately, although mechanical clocks began to appear in the thirteenth century they were neither very reliable, nor capable of being used at sea. Even Galileo's invention of the pendulum in 1602, which gave a new precision to clocks ashore, was no help to seamen; despite many trials the movement of the ship made such clocks useless to them. We will come back later to the vital question of determining the time at sea, which now, of course, is no problem at all. For the moment we will end the story by noting that in 1714 the British Government set up a special Board of Longitude empowered to give a prize of £20,000—a staggering sum for those days—to anybody demonstrating a way of determining longitude at sea to within half a degree. The ultimate winner, in 1772, was John Harrison (1693–1776) whose famous spring-driven watch is now preserved in the National Maritime Museum, Greenwich. A replica of this watch was taken, for test purposes, by James Cook on his second and third voyages. An entry in Cook's log for the *Resolution* and *Adventure* records that after a voyage of just over three years the error of the watch on arrival at Portsmouth was less than 17 minutes of arc.

For the moment, however, we must go back to Magellan and his successors; their arduous voyages gradually built up a general picture of the Pacific which was to be dramatically extended, and furnished with detail, by James Cook. For them, the only

19

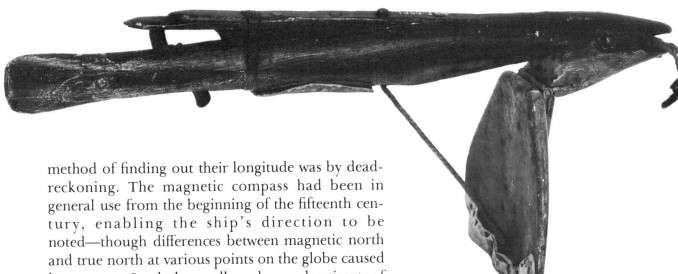

method of finding out their longitude was by dead-reckoning. The magnetic compass had been in general use from the beginning of the fifteenth century, enabling the ship's direction to be noted—though differences between magnetic north and true north at various points on the globe caused large errors. Sand-glasses allowed a rough estimate of how long the ship sailed in a particular direction; they were used also for timing the watches. The ship's speed through the water could be judged quite well by eye. Later, towards the end of the sixteenth century, the log was introduced to measure speed more accurately. The log was a board so weighted that when thrown into the sea it floated upright. Attached to the board was a long line knotted at intervals. The log was thrown overboard, and its high resistance to the water made it remain almost stationary as the ship drew away. As the line was paid out, the seaman counted the number of knots that ran through his hand in a given interval of time, measured by a sand-glass. In theory, therefore, a ship's position could be determined by regularly recording its course and speed. In practice, many things upset the calculation. Cross-winds and currents could throw things out badly.

As new discoveries were made they were put into maps and charts, but only slowly: the map-makers were reluctant to make the expensive new printing plates. But these new details could be dangerously inaccurate. A big problem was how to project the surface of the spherical earth on to a flat sheet of paper. On the ordinary "plain charts" the north-south lines were parallel, although in fact they converge towards the poles. So, if the distance between places was cor-

Above A ship's wooden log used to measure speed through the water.

rect, then the compass bearing from one to the other was wrong, and *vice versa*. Not until 1569 did Mercator (1512–94) issue his chart of the world solving this by a mathematical device now known as Mercator's projection.

One other important piece of equipment was the lead-line, which served a dual purpose. Apart from showing the depth of water, it usually carried a piece of tallow, to which mud, gravel and the like would stick; this gave the seaman some idea of the nature of the sea-floor below him.

We know from contemporary records what navigational aids Magellan had. There were twenty-one quadrants, seven marine astrolabes, thirty-seven compass needles, eighteen sand-glasses, and twenty-three charts. His immediate successors were scarcely

Below left Gerard Mercator (1512–94), Flemish mathematician, geographer and map-maker whose device for presenting a map of a spherical surface on flat paper solved a number of problems encountered by earlier cartographers. *Below right* One of Mercator's maps of the southern hemisphere.

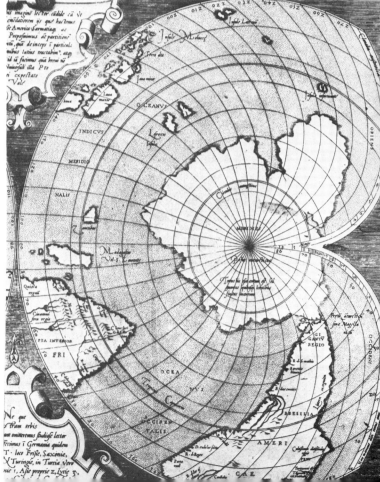

better equipped, and so just as uncertain of their whereabouts. As a result, there followed a long period of frustrating uncertainty. Landfalls were made but there was no way of finding them again. Sometimes, it is now clear, places were rediscovered and given quite different names and locations. Even today, we cannot identify some of the places described.

In Mexico, Spain had an ambitious and forceful governor in Hernando Cortes (1485–1547), who had been appointed in 1522. Cortes was anxious to exploit Magellan's success, and sent out several expeditions but they had little success; some were lost and never heard of again. One, under Alvaro de Saavedra, dispatched in 1527, reached the Moluccas and in the course of two unsuccessful attempts to beat their way back to Mexico, explored the north coast of New Guinea.

The first major discovery was that of the Hawaiian group of islands in 1555 by Juan Gaetano, but no less important for the future of Pacific exploration was one made two years later by Andres de Urdaneta; he made his way back to Mexico by going northwards and there finding steady westerly winds like those of the north Atlantic. This discovery coincided with the founding of a Spanish colony in the Philippines. If a ship left the capital, Manila, in June it could expect to arrive back at Acapulco in Mexico within six months; this was much longer than the outward journey, but perfectly feasible. On this basis a regular crossing of the Pacific was established. While this cut a broad swathe across the ocean, this was so vast that still only a tiny fraction of it was explored. Gradually more was learned about winds and currents and by 1709 William Dampier was able to codify this in a chapter on "A View of the General and Coasting Trade Winds in the Great Southern Ocean" in his *Discussion of Winds*.

Hernando Cortes finally left Mexico in 1540, and the centre of Pacific exploration shifted to Callao in

A sixteenth century Spanish painting of the landing in Mexico in 1519 of Hernando Cortes.

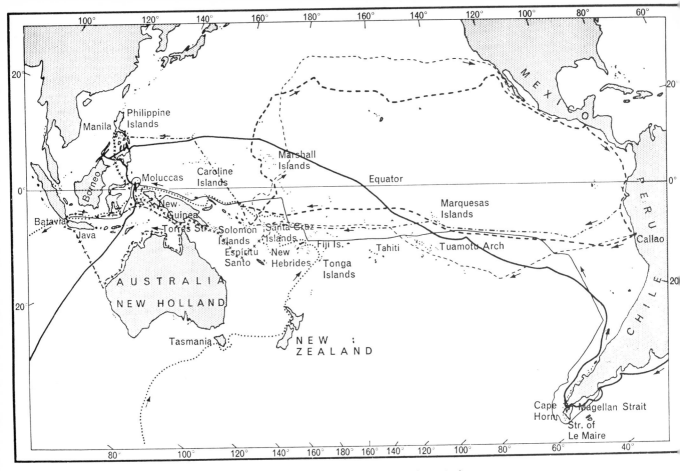

Voyages of exploration in the South Pacific: sixteenth and seventeenth centuries.

Magellan 1520–22 ——————— Mendaña 1567–69 — — — — — Mendaña and Quiros 1595–96 — · — · — ·
Quiros and Torres 1605–6 - - - - - - - - Torres xxxxxxxx Schouten and Le Maire 1615–16 ———————
Tasman 1642–43 ····················· Tasman 1644 — x — x —

Peru, where the Spaniards dreamed of a great oceanic empire as rich as either Mexico or Peru, whose pagan inhabitants might be brought within the Christian fold. They were encouraged by an Incan legend of a rich land some 2,000 miles to the west. The Viceroy of Peru sent two expeditions in search of this under his nephew Alvaro de Mendaña. The first, in 1567, took them to the Solomon Islands, from which they struggled back to Callao after two years' absence. On his next voyage (1595) Mendaña could not find the Solomon Islands again, and confused them with the Marquesas, at only half the distance. In fact, the Solomons were not visited again for nearly two cen-

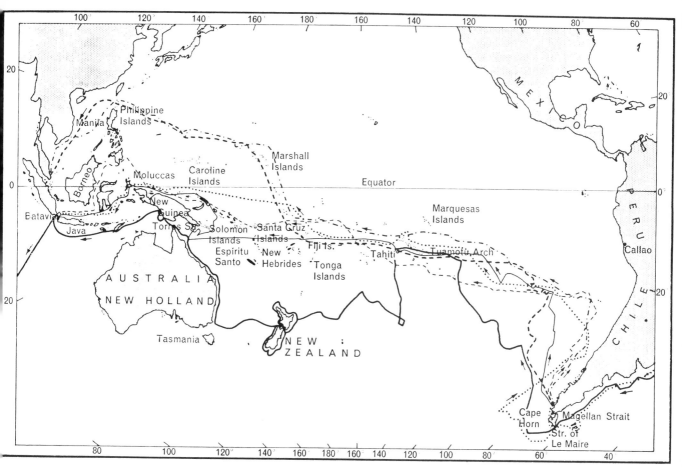

Voyages of exploration in the South Pacific: eighteenth century.

Roggeveen 1721–22 ····················   Byron 1764–65 — · — · — ·   Wallis 1766–67 — — — — —

Carteret 1766–68 – – – – – – –   Bougainville 1767–68 ———————   Cook 1768–71 ———————

turies, this time by Bougainville in 1767, who did not identify them with those described by Mendaña. Two years later Jean de Surville made the same mistake. Such was the uncertainty of Pacific exploration! At last, Mendaña made his way to Santa Cruz, where he died. The expedition was at last brought home, by way of the New Hebrides, by his skilful navigator Pedro de Quiros. Quiros mistakenly believed the New Hebrides to be the much-sought southern continent. He called it *Austrialia del Esperitu Santo*, which James Cook sought and found on his second voyage. Quiros' second-in-command was Luis de Torres, who went home by himself in another ship. In this he touched at New Guinea and sailed through the great strait to the south of it which now bears his name. He thus cleared up one major geographical problem: New Guinea was not part of a southern continent.

For half a century after Ferdinand Magellan, the Spaniards had the Pacific more or less to themselves and they said little about their discoveries. Their complacency was rudely shaken by Francis Drake who with a little fleet of five vessels—headed by the 100-ton *Pelican*, later the *Golden Hind*—made a circumnavigation that began at Plymouth on 13th December, 1577, and ended on 26th September, 1580. Drake's historic voyage was not basically one of exploration, but one of piracy. It is said that no British ship had ever returned home with a richer cargo.

Nevertheless, it did add much to knowledge of the Pacific. After passing through the Straits of Magellan, storms drove him southward to sight Cape Horn where "The Atlanticke Ocean and the South Sea meete in a most large and free scope." Of a southern continent there was no sign. Originally Drake had proposed coming home by the Straits of Magellan, but he would have risked capture by the Spaniards. So he decided to try another route provided for in his sailing orders, namely to return by way of the so-called Straits of Anian, which were supposed to give access to a passage to the north of America. In the event, Drake could find no such strait even at 48°N, so he returned and refitted on the California coast. Thence he returned home via a westward route, calling at the Moluccas. If the Straits of Anian existed, Drake had shown that they were much further north than people had thought.

Akin to Drake was William Dampier (1652–1715) whose aim was also plunder rather than exploration. He, too, made a circumnavigation described in his *Voyage round the World* (1697). Later (1699–1700) he went back to the Pacific, and explored the coasts of

Above The *Pelican* in which Drake sailed round the world, 1577–80. After sailing through the Straits of Magellan he renamed his ship the *Golden Hind*.

Above Sir Francis Drake (c. 1540–96), the greatest of Elizabethan seamen and scourge of the Spanish and Portuguese navies. *Below* Drake's dial, a magnificent combination of navigational instruments which was made in brass in 1569.

27

north-west Australia, New Guinea, and New Britain.

By this time, the Dutch too were becoming interested, and three big expeditions set out in search of the elusive southern continent. Their ships were more seaworthy than those of Spain and they made regular use of the back-staff for navigation. The first expedition, in 1615, was led by William Schouten and Jacob Le Maire, who came by way of Cape Horn. They made their way to Java, and lost their ship there; they had found various islands, but no continent. No better luck was had by Abel Tasman, sent out by the East India Company, who in 1642 entered the Pacific from the west. He discovered Tasmania and the west coast of New Zealand; he thought this might have been part of a continent, though James Cook later

Abel Tasman's encounter with Maoris on his discovery of New Zealand in 1642. Later that same year he discovered what is now known as Tasmania, though he named it Van Diemen's Land after the governor-general of the Dutch settlement in Batavia.

disproved this by sailing right round it. Jacob Rogge-veen, under the auspices of the Dutch West India Company, entered the Pacific in 1721 and followed roughly in the path of Magellan: he discovered Samoa and Easter Island, both interesting, but of a continent he, too, saw no sign.

At the beginning of the seventeenth century a lot of uncertainty about the Pacific had been dispelled. What one might call the midriff of the ocean had been quite well traversed. At the same time, there still remained in the south-west an unexplored area vast enough to contain a new continent if one did indeed exist. The philosophers still believed in it and governments—especially those of France and Britain, now in the ascendant—were not sceptical enough to deny the possibility. Pacific expeditions were costly, but should one find a new continent the investment could prove hugely profitable. It was in this climate of opinion that a number of naval expeditions were dis-patched in the 1760s.

Of these expeditions, two—which effectively became three—were British. The first (1764–6) was led by John Byron, who was given two main objec-tives. Firstly, he was to seek land in the extreme south Atlantic; secondly, he was to proceed into the Pacific and try, like Drake, to find a passage around North America to Hudson's Bay. The last should have been a big temptation, for in 1745 the British Parliament had offered a prize of £20,000 to the first British citizen to make such a passage in a British vessel. Surprisingly, Byron seems to have made little effort to do this. Instead, he, too, sailed westward across the Pacific's midriff, finding some new islands on the way. Even-tually he reached the Ladrones and then made his way to Batavia by sailing north of the Philippines. He came home a year and eleven months after setting out—the fastest circumnavigation yet made, but one not otherwise very fruitful.

Two years later, John Byron was followed by

John Byron's meeting with the inhabitants of one of the islands he visited on his Pacific voyage.

Oberea, the Queen of Tahiti, surrendering the islands to Captain Samuel Wallis—in 1767. Wallis's reception at the islands was quite hostile but by the time the *Dolphin* and its crew were ready to leave, their "Indian friends", Wallis tells us, said goodbye "with such tenderness of affection and grief, as filled both my heart and my eyes."

Samuel Wallis, in the *Dolphin*, who had as his companion Philip Carteret in the *Swallow*. The two vessels became separated during one of the most arduous passages through the Straits of Magellan ever recorded, no less than four months battling with violent tempests. The *Dolphin* was unable to turn back to look for the *Swallow*, which was presumed lost, and after passing into the Pacific set a northerly course to about the Tropic of Capricorn. There Wallis turned westward and took a course not very different from that of John Byron, and with no more startling results. Among his discoveries was Tahiti, whose position he accurately charted. Tahiti was to be Cook's first destination in the Pacific.

Meanwhile, Philip Carteret was battling on in his wake, despite the fact that the *Swallow* was so unseaworthy that she ought never to have set out on so arduous a voyage. He, too, made his way north to the Tropic of Capricorn and then made his way west by a route rather to the south of Byron's. Eventually he, too, made his way to Batavia and thence safe home to Britain via the Cape.

On the last leg of his voyage home, Carteret was overtaken by a French naval vessel, the *Boudeuse* under the command of Louis de Bougainville, who was able to tell him that the *Dolphin* had returned safely. He did not disclose that he, too, was completing a voyage of circumnavigation that had started in 1767. Bougainville, too, found his way to Tahiti, and unknowingly did James Cook a valuable service by making friendly contact with its inhabitants. Thence he sailed almost due west until finally he reached what we now know as the Great Barrier Reef of Australia (New Holland), on which Cook later nearly came to grief. He did not, and could not, realize that he had touched on a vast island—though still not the long-sought southern continent; like William Dampier, he was inclined to regard New Holland as a collection of islands. From there he went on to the Solomon Islands, which he

failed to identify with those of Mendaña, and to
Batavia, going home by the Cape. He had made
several new discoveries, but a great southern continent was not among them. Even so, these great cir-
cumnavigations of the 1760s still left unexplored an
area in the south Pacific large enough to contain it. It
was left to Cook finally to prove that no such continent existed.

Louis de Bougainville's voyage was very important
to Cook, and oddly the two men's paths had crossed
many years before. Bougainville had been *aide-de-
camp* to Montcalm during the siege of Quebec, while
Cook was serving in a British vessel on the St.
Lawrence River. With Bougainville there sailed a
young French astronomer, Pierre Véron, whose job
was to work out longitude during the voyage. We have
already noted that early explorers had been wildly
wrong over this, but meanwhile science had ad-
vanced, and a considerable degree of accuracy at-
tained. The ultimate solution was to be the marine
chronometer, but meanwhile other alternatives had
been explored.

One, based on the motions and eclipses of the
satellites of Jupiter, had been developed by Galileo
following his observation of these satellites in 1609 by
means of the newly invented telescope. It was a
method to which Cook was much attracted but it
needed a long rigidly mounted telescope and
elaborate computations, so it was no good for use at
sea. However, with the aid of tables published by the
Paris Observatory in the late eighteenth century, a
good astronomer could determine longitude to
within a degree or so if he could establish a land base
in fair weather.

Another method was that of lunars, based upon
observing the position of the moon. Again, a very
elaborate calculation was needed, but the back of this
was broken by the aid of tables published in *The
Nautical Almanac*, the first edition of which appeared in

Above Louis Antoine de Bougainville
(1729–1811), the French navigator whose
voyage round the world, 1776–79, was the
first that the French accomplished.

32

Top left John Hadley's reflecting quadrant (so-called—it was really an octant), devised in 1731, overcame the problems caused by the ship's motion by using the principle of double reflection.

Right A sextant—a refinement of the octant which is still used today.

1767, the year before James Cook began his voyage in the *Endeavour*. Even so, the calculation might take several hours. But the reward—a determination of longitude reliable within one degree—made such labour vastly worthwhile. For the first time, the Pacific explorers—and mariners generally—could pinpoint their discoveries, so that they or others could find them again. In 1781, no less than 10,000 copies of the *Almanac* were sold. It would, however, have been useless without the means of making the astronomical observations at sea with sufficient accuracy. For this, navigators were indebted to John Hadley (1682–1744), who in 1731 invented the reflecting octant, ancestor of the sextant, devised by Captain John Campbell in 1757. On his first voyage Cook navigated by lunars; not until the second did he have the benefit of Harrison's marine chronometer, still at an experimental stage.

In the century and a half since Ferdinand Magellan the Pacific had lost much, but by no means all, of its mystery. The time was ripe for truly scientific voyages of exploration and in James Cook there proved to be a man uniquely qualified to lead them. To his life and achievements we must now return in detail.

THE

NAUTICAL ALMANAC

AND

ASTRONOMICAL EPHEMERIS,

FOR THE YEAR 1767.

Published by ORDER of the

COMMISSIONERS OF LONGITUDE.

LONDON:

Printed by W. RICHARDSON and S. CLARK, PRINTERS;

AND SOLD BY

J. NOURSE, in the Strand, and Meſſ. MOUNT and PAGE, on Tower-Hill,

Bookſellers to the ſaid COMMISSIONERS.

M DCC LXVI.

The title page of the first edition of *The Nautical Almanac* of 1767. It has been published annually ever since.

2 Cook's Early Life

James Cook was born at Marton-in-Cleveland, a small Yorkshire village some twenty miles from Whitby, on 27th October, 1728. His father was a farm worker of Scottish descent and his only formal education was such as the village school could supply. At the age of twelve he was apprenticed to a draper in the nearby fishing village of Staithes. It was here, perhaps, that he first felt the lure of the sea that was to prove his great passion. After a short time the boy left the shop and became apprenticed to John Walker, a coal-shipper in Whitby, whose business was mainly with the local mines. With him he did well, and he learned the rudiments of seamanship on coastal voyages and on longer ones to Norway and the Baltic. In his spare time James studied Euclid and the principles of

The two-room cottage in Marton-in-Cleveland, Yorkshire, where James Cook was born in 1728.

navigating. By the age of twenty-four he had risen to the rank of mate and could shortly have expected to be entrusted with a command of his own by his employer.

In 1755, however, international disputes gave his career a new course. In 1740, Prussia had seized Silesia from Austria and so became embroiled with that country, Russia, and France; this culminated in the Seven Years' War of 1756–63. In this conflict, Britain found herself once again opposed to France. In the previous year there had been some naval skirmishes with the French and in 1755 James Cook—perhaps as a deliberate move towards a naval career, perhaps to forestall the press gang—enlisted as an able seaman in the Royal Navy. He was appointed to the *Eagle*, a 60-gun vessel commanded by Captain Hugh Palliser, also a Yorkshireman. It is said that Cook had been recommended to him by the Member of Parliament for Scarborough; whether this is true or not, Palliser soon recognized Cook's worth and took an active interest in his career: after four years he gained his warrant as master. This was an important promotion, for the master was directly responsible, under the captain, for the navigation and handling of the ship.

In this new capacity he was appointed to the *Mercury* in 1759 and sent to North America. His task was to make a detailed survey of the St. Lawrence River as part of the pending operations against Quebec. He carried it out well enough to attract the attention of Sir Charles Saunders, commander-in-chief of the St. Lawrence fleet, and he was awarded a special gratuity of £50. On Saunders' return to England after the fall of Quebec in 1759, Cook was made master of the *Northumberland*, the command of Lord Colville who was then the senior officer. During these years, he spent much of his free time improving his knowledge of mathematics and navigation, and made a special study of astronomical navigation. He learned much

Captain Hugh Palliser (1723–1825), under whom Cook served for four years in the *Eagle*. Palliser supported the nomination of Cook to head the expedition to the Pacific to observe the transit of Venus.

from the famous military surveyor Samuel Holland. In 1762, he made a detailed survey of the harbour of Placentia in Newfoundland, and this added further to his reputation.

By this time he was thirty-four years old, and recognized not only as a thoroughly capable seaman but as a gifted surveyor and navigator. His career seemed assured, and on his return to England in 1762 he married Elizabeth Batts, of Shadwell, some fourteen years his junior. Of their married life we know little, but like the wives of many naval officers, Elizabeth had to put up with long absences by her husband. Her family was to prove small comfort to her. Of their six children, three died in infancy, and the other three she long outlived. Nathaniel, aged only sixteen, was lost in the *Thunderer* in the West Indies in 1780. Hugh died at Cambridge, aged only a year older. The eldest, James, rose to command the *Spitfire* but was drowned in a gale in 1794. Elizabeth herself lived on until 1835, dying in her ninety-fourth year.

In 1763 Hugh Palliser went back to North America as Governor of Newfoundland and this led to Cook being appointed Marine Surveyor of the Coast of Newfoundland and Labrador. Much importance attached to this: apart from their intrinsic importance, the Newfoundland fisheries were a principal training ground for seamen for the Navy. These duties occupied him for the next four years, during which he was given command of a sloop, the *Grenville*. His routine was to use the good summer months for surveying, and the winter ones to see about the publication of his results in England. The final result was a series of volumes (1766–68) of sailing directions of notable clarity and accuracy.

During these four years there occurred a natural phenomenon of no little significance for Cook's future career. In 1766, an eclipse of the sun was visible in Newfoundland and astronomical observations of

Whatever the truth in the suggestion that Cook enlisted in the Navy to forestall the press gang, press gangs were very much in evidence, especially in wartime. This cartoon, from the *Oxford Magazine,* 1770 is entitled "The Press Gang or English Liberty Display'd."

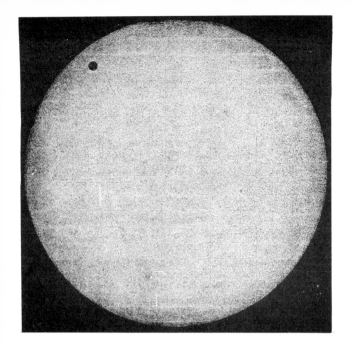

this were made by Cook at Cape Ray. The results were sent to the Royal Society in London, and published in their *Transactions* in 1767. Cook was thus firmly on record as both a skilful navigator and a capable practical astronomer. His name naturally came forward when in June, 1766, the Royal Society began to turn its attention to the observation of another astronomical phenomenon; this was the transit of Venus, which would be visible in the Pacific in June, 1769. Accurate observations of this event were of great scientific value, for they would provide a precise means of calculating the distance of the earth from the sun. A reliable and skilful observer was essential, as there would not be another chance for over a century if this one were missed—not until 1874, in fact. The Royal Society sent a petition to George III requesting funds to pay for an expedition, and these were quickly forthcoming. We shall see later that governmental enthusiasm was not solely the result of a desire to advance scientific knowledge.

Initially, the Royal Society had wanted to entrust the expedition to Alexander Dalrymple, who had made a special study of existing knowledge of the

Above Alexander Dalrymple (1737–1825), the Scottish hydrographer who had strong backing to lead the expedition into the Pacific.

Above right The Royal Society's houses in Crane Court, Fleet Street, which were its quarters from 1710 until it moved to Somerset House in 1780.

Pacific and firmly believed in a great southern continent. It was a reasonable enough choice, and his ability as a surveyor was later to be recognized by his appointment as the first hydrographer to the Navy. The Astronomer Royal, Nevil Maskelyne, backed Dalrymple, he "having a particular turn for discoveries and being an able navigator and well skilled in observations." However, an insuperable difficulty arose. On being approached, Dalrymple would accept only if he had "the total management of the ship intended to be sent." This was, not surprisingly, quite unacceptable to the Admiralty: the First Lord, Edward Hawke, said he would sooner have his right hand cut off than sign such a commission. Dalrymple refused to climb down, and so the Royal Society had to recommend someone else. It was in these circumstances that Cook's name came forward as that of a commander acceptable to both the Admiralty and the Royal Society. He was then in London and took the command in May 1768, with the rank of lieutenant; it was agreed that he should receive a gratuity of 100 guineas for carrying out the astronomical observations.

3 *The* Endeavour *Voyage*

It is often said, plausibly enough, that Cook chose the *Endeavour* because she was a Whitby collier, a vessel whose good sea-going qualities he knew well. This kind of ship could be beached on an almost even keel for repairs far away from dockyard facilities. In fact, this pleasing story is untrue. Although Cook was certainly well enough pleased with the choice, his name did not come before the Admiralty until April, 1768, some weeks after instructions had been given to find a suitable vessel. Several were examined in the River Thames, including one named the *Earl of Pembroke*, a typical north-east collier; she was surveyed on 23rd March and bought for £2,000 only a few days later. She was to be registered in the Navy as the bark *Endeavour*. She was a vessel of modest size: a little over 100 feet in length overall, and of 369 tons burthen.

The *Endeavour* was taken at once to Deptford dockyard for a thorough overhaul. Since much had to be done, and she was to sail in July, the work was given high priority. She was sheathed in new planks, heavily studded with iron nails to discourage the highly destructive Teredo worm of tropical seas. At the same time, the masts and rigging were largely renewed and some armaments installed; apart from hand weapons, there were six four-pounder guns and twelve swivel-guns.

While this was going on a normal crew had to be mustered, as well as such additional members as the special nature of the voyage made necessary. It will be remembered that Cook himself was going to make the scientific observations of the transit of Venus that were the outward reason for the expedition; to help him he had a young astronomer, Charles Green, who was assistant to the Astronomer Royal at Greenwich. In

Left The bark *Endeavour* which Cook commanded on his first voyage to the South Pacific. This pen drawing is taken from a painting by R. Langmaid, which was based on all available data.

Below The Teredo worm, commonly known as the shipworm. They can cause considerable damage to ships' timber and to woodwork in harbours, burrowing along the grain and breeding very rapidly.

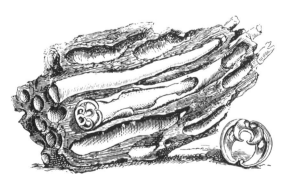

addition, other scientific investigations were to be made, especially into the natural history of the Pacific. For this purpose, there was added to the party a young botanist, Joseph Banks, with seven assistants.

So far as the scientific consequences of the *Endeavour* voyage are concerned, Banks's contribution was so great that we must say something of him. The son of a wealthy family—he inherited a very large fortune when he came of age in 1764—he chose to devote his life to the study of botany. On graduating from Oxford in 1763, he sailed as a naturalist on the *Niger*, a Fishery Protection vessel sailing to Newfoundland and Labrador. Returning to London, as a newly elected Fellow of the Royal Society, he learned of the proposed voyage to the Pacific and at once saw what a big chance this would give him for the study of a fauna and flora that was still virtually unknown. The Royal Society commended him to the Admiralty, and the latter agreed to accept him and his party. Chief among these was Daniel Solander, a Swede who had studied under Linnaeus, the great Swedish botanist. He had come to London and had been appointed naturalist at the British Museum; he, too, was a Fellow of the Royal Society and regarded as one of the

Above left Sir Joseph Banks (1744–1820) by Sir Joshua Reynolds (1723–92), painted after Banks's return from the *Endeavour* voyage when he was about thirty years old. *Above* Daniel Solander (1736–82), the Swedish student and follower of the renowned botanist Carl Linnaeus (1707–78). At Joseph Banks's expense he sailed on the *Endeavour*.

ablest botanists of his day. With them went five assistants—three of them artists—to help in collecting, describing, and drawing material. Of this party it was rightly said that "No people ever went to sea better fitted out for the purpose of Natural History. They have got a fine library . . .; they have all sorts of machines for catching and preserving insects; all kinds of nets, trawls, drags, and hooks for coral fishing . . . even a curious contrivance of a telescope by which . . . you can see the bottom at a great depth." The cost of all this was £10,000, the whole of which was paid for by Banks himself. The addition of Banks' party, together with twelve marines, brought the complement to 85, a lot for so small a vessel. Quarters were cramped, but on the whole harmony prevailed; in particular, Cook, Banks, and Solander—a very diverse trio—got on well from the outset.

We will come back to the scientific achievements of the voyage in a later chapter. For the moment, we will record only that it made Banks a scientific celebrity and a personal friend of George III. In 1778 he was elected President of the Royal Society, and held this important office for no less than forty-one years, during which he dominated the scientific scene in Britain. In his later years he played a leading role in establishing Kew Gardens, one of the world's most famous botanical gardens; he helped to establish the tea plant in India; he introduced the Merino sheep into Britain from Spain; and he took an interest in founding the first British colony in Australia at Botany Bay in 1788. George III made him a baronet in 1781.

The *Endeavour* finally sailed from Plymouth on 25th August, 1768. Her initial destination was Tahiti, where the crucial astronomical observations were to be made. With him, however, James Cook took secret orders, dated a month previously, which plainly show that the Lords of the Admiralty were by no means concerned only with the transit of Venus and the scientific study of the plant and animal life of the Pacific. Additionally, Cook was told to make a systematic search for the supposed great southern continent:

"Whereas there is reason to imagine that a Continent or Land of great extent may be found to the Southward of the Tract lately made by Capt. Wallis in His Majesty's Ship the Dolphin . . . or of the Tract of any former Navigators in pursuits of the like kind; You are therefore in Pursuance of His Majesty's Pleasure hereby required and directed to put to Sea with the Bark you Command so soon as the Observation of the Transit of the Planet Venus shall be finished . . ."

Samuel Wallis had, in fact, come back to England on 20th May, 1768, so Cook could be given all the details of his voyage.

Briefly, Cook's further instructions were to sail south from Tahiti until he reached latitude 40°S. He was then to turn westward between that latitude and 35°S until he either found the supposed continent or reached New Zealand, which Abel Tasman had discovered. In the latter case, he was to survey the coast of New Zealand as thoroughly as he could and then come home via the Cape of Good Hope or Cape Horn. If he found the continent he was to take possession of it with the consent of the natives; if uninhabited, he was to "set up Proper Marks and Inscriptions, as first discoverers and possessors." He was to do the same with other new territories not previously discovered by Europeans.

The secret nature of this part of his mission was underlined in two ways. Firstly, at the end of the voyage Cook was to impound any log-books and journals his officers might have made, and the entire crew was to be forbidden to say where they had been, until permission was given. Secondly, Cook took with him an Admiralty warrant requiring all British ships with whom he might fall in to give him all possible

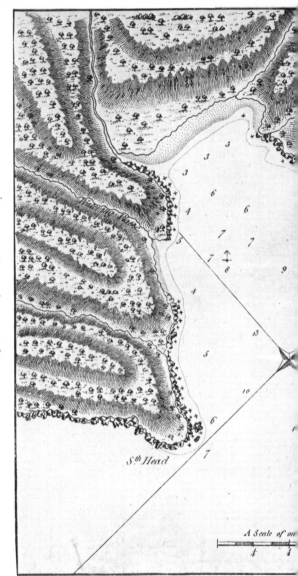

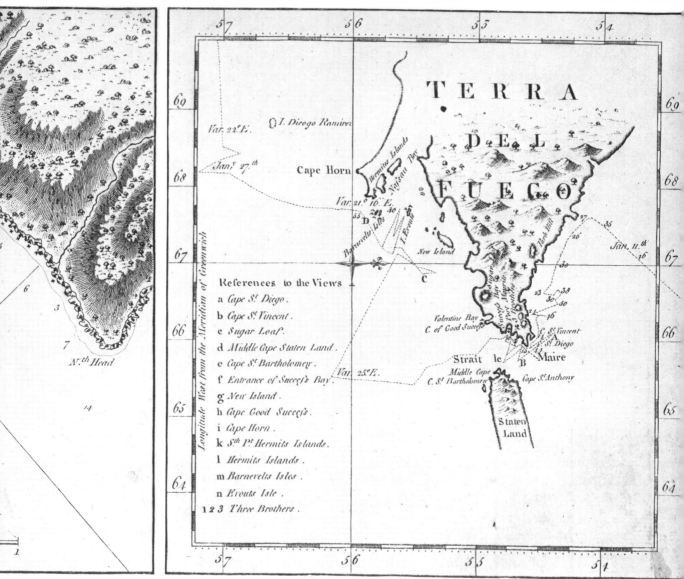

Left A plan of the Bay of Success and *right* a chart of the south-east part of Tierra del Fuego by Captain Cook, 1769.

assistance; they were not, however, entitled to demand of him a sight of "the Instructions he has received from us."

By the standards of the day, the voyage to Tahiti was uneventful. Following his instructions, Cook entered the Pacific by way of Cape Horn. On 11th December Tierra del Fuego was sighted and four days later the *Endeavour* anchored in the Bay of Success. Banks and Solander, eager to miss no chance of botanizing, took a party ashore but were unlucky enough to be overtaken by a blizzard. The botanists were none the

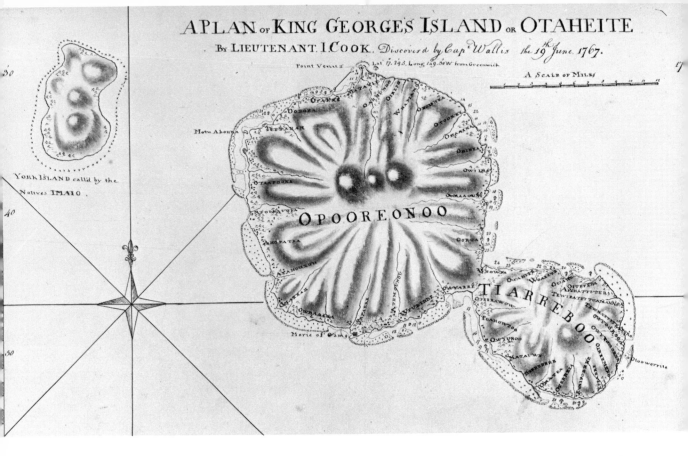

A PLAN of KING GEORGES ISLAND or OTAHEITE

By LIEUTENANT. I. COOK. Discover'd by Cap.ᵗ Wallis the 19ᵗʰ June. 1767.

Point Venus Lat. 17.29 S. Long. 149.30 W from Greenwich

A SCALE OF MILES

YORK ISLAND call'd by the
Natives IMAIO

OPOOREONOO

TIARREBOO

Cook's plan of Tahiti, which he reached in
the *Endeavour* at the end of January 1769.

worse, but two negro servants were frozen to death.
On 30th January, 1769, the ship turned northward
and on 13th April—well in advance of the transit of
Venus—anchored at Tahiti in Matavai Bay, which
Samuel Wallis had used. Characteristically, Cook
used part of the time to make an accurate survey of the
island.

The natives were friendly but—as all other Pacific
explorers had found—inveterate and extraordinarily
ingenious thieves. One item stolen was the
astronomical quadrant, but luckily it was soon
recovered. It had been damaged, but by good fortune
Banks' lavish equipment included "a Set of Watch
Makers Tools & These Happy Circumstances [made]
all Easy again!" Thieving was not limited to the
natives. The women were very free with their favours
with the crew but expected to be paid—a favourite
currency was iron nails taken from the ship's store.

A view of Tahiti, showing several native craft.

On one occasion, a crew member was given two dozen lashes for this offence. Wallis had recorded a similar—indeed worse—experience: his crew became so desperate for nails that they even began to extract them from the hull!

An observatory and small fort were set up ashore and the transit of Venus was observed in perfect weather on 3rd June. Independent observations were made by Cook, Charles Green, and Daniel Solander.

Cook always showed an inquiring mind. Apart from making his astronomical observations, surveying the island and obtaining details of more than a hundred others nearby, he made, and wrote in his log, many detailed notes on the religious and social customs of the natives. By early August, however, all this had been done, after a stay of almost four months, and on 9th August he set sail southward on the next stage of his voyage.

Southwards he continued as far as 40°, when bad weather prevented him going further. He saw no land and, to a practised seaman, the heavy swell from the south was a sign of open sea for a long way. He therefore turned westward, as instructed, and at the end of September began to see signs of land—birds flying near the ship and the debris of land floating in the sea. On 9th October he anchored in a bay on the north island of New Zealand. He failed to establish friendly relations with the natives—several were killed in a fracas—and could obtain no provisions. Disappointed, he called it Poverty Bay (now the site of Gisborne) and turned south again along the coast un-

A Maori war canoe, engraved after a drawing by Sydney Parkinson (c. 1745–71) the most productive artist on the first voyage. The Maoris were unfriendly and a number were killed in fighting that broke out more than once.

til he reached Cape Turnagain at 40°S. Some fresh food was obtained and Joseph Banks and Daniel Solander acquired many specimens. Then he turned north again, past Cape Poverty, and round the East Cape into the great Bay of Plenty. On 9th November he and Charles Green landed to observe a transit of Mercury; at this point, Mercury Bay, plentiful wood , water, and fresh provisions were obtained. Here Cook formally took possession of the whole country.

Proceeding north, he rounded North Cape in a tempest, and then worked his way south until, at the beginning of February, he reached the famous strait that now bears his name. Going on, he reached Cape

Turnagain once more, this time from the south, and so conclusively proved that this part of New Zealand was an island. From natives, he learned that the land to the south of Cook Strait formed part of a similar island, which too he circumnavigated and charted.

Quite clearly, New Zealand, though a sizeable territory, was not part of a great southern continent. In the course of six months 2,400 miles of its coast had been surveyed with remarkable accuracy. The only minor doubt, due to bad weather, was whether Stewart Island at the extreme southern tip might not in fact be a peninsula. In all, it was a fine achievement and one that would alone have made the expedition a notable success.

Cook, however, had by no means finished. It was tempting to try to return by Cape Horn in a high southern latitude—as his instructions permitted—and so eliminate the possibility of a southern continent in that unexplored region. On balance,

Above One of the many "Natural Curiosities" that were discovered in New Zealand was the Perforated Rock in Tolaga Bay.

Right Cook's chart (engraved by I. Bayly) of New Zealand as explored in 1769 and 1770, showing the course of the *Endeavour* round the two islands.

CHART
of
NEW-ZEALAND,
explored in 1769 and 1770,
- by -
Lieut: I. COOK, Commander
of
His Majesty's Bark
ENDEAVOUR.

Engrav'd by I. Bayly.

EXPLANATION

The ffrickd lines ffews the Ships Track,
and the figures annexd the depth of Water
in fathoms.
The unffnifh'd part of the Coast, has not
been explored.
♈ places where the Ships Anchor'd.
. Rocks above Water.
. Rocks under Water.
Var. &c. ffews the Compafs East Variation
in Degrees and Minutes.
In Cook's Strait, the Flood fide comes ftrong
in from the Southward, and on the days of the
New and Full Moon is High-water about 11
o'Clock.

A Scale of Leagues 20 to a Degree.

Three Kings
Cape Maria Van Diemen
NORTH CAPE
M. Camel
C. BRETT
Poor Knights
Bream Head
Hen and Chickens
Bream Bay
Bream Tail
Ps Rodney
False Bay
THE DESERT COAST
RIVER THAMES
Mercury Ifles
MERCURY BAY
Onetonga
Court of Aldermen
The Mayor
White Ifld
C RUNAWAY
BAY of PLENTY
C EAST
East Ifl.
Broken Isles
Town
Low Land Point
High Land pt
Mount Edgcumbe
Tegadoo
Tolaga
Spring Ifl.
POVERTY BAY or TAONEROA
Young Nick's Hd
Cape End Van land
Ientan-metti
EAHEINOMAUWE
Gunnet Ifle
Woody Head
Albatrofs Point
T A B L E C A P E
Terakako
Teahowray
HAWKE'S BAY
Sugar loaf Ifles
Sugar loaf Point
CAPE EGMONT
Mount Egmont
C. KIDNAPPERS
Black Head
C. Turnagain

Left the Coast
COOK'S
CAPE FAREWELL
Blind Bay
Rocks Point
ADMIRALTY BAY
QUEEN CHARLOTTE'S SOUND
Two Brothers
Castle Pt
Flat Pt
CAPE FOUL-WIND
Cloudy Bay
CAPE CAMPBEL
CAPE PALLISSER
STRAITS

POENAMMOO
SNOWEY MOUNTAINS
Lookers on
Gores Bay
BANKS'S ISLAND

Cafcades Point
Miftaken Bay
T. AVAI POENAMMOO
THE SOUTH
C. SAUNDERS

Doubtful Harb'
Five Fingers Point
Dufkey Bay
WEST CAPE
SOLANDER'S ISLE
S.W. Bay
Molineux's Harb'
S.E. Bay
Bench Ifl'd
CAPE SOUTH
The Traps

Longitude Weft from the Meridian of Greenwich.

The inside of a hippah—or fortified Maori encampment—in New Zealand.

however, he thought this too hazardous at that season—it was now March, 1770—and instead he decided to go westward once more until he struck the coast of New Holland (Australia) and survey as much as he could of its east coast. In the event, this choice was to put him in as great peril as the attempt to return eastward could have done, but of this he and his party were happily ignorant.

On the last day of March he left New Zealand and on 19th April, 1770, made his landfall on the west of

Australia; it was another ten days, however, before a safe anchorage was found. This was Botany Bay—so called because of the wealth of new material found by the botanists—which was later to be the site of the first British colony in Australia. Following his intention, he sailed steadily northward surveying the coast and collecting specimens.

This devotion to surveying brought the expedition to near disaster, for by keeping close inshore Cook actually sailed within the Great Barrier Reef. Despite

every precaution, the *Endeavour* went hard aground on a coral reef late on the night of 11th May. Unfortunately, she struck at high water, so there was no chance of floating her off on the tide, supposing she was not too badly damaged. The only hope was to lighten her and during the night some fifty tons of gear was thrown overboard—ballast, guns, decayed stores, and much else. Nevertheless, at the next high water she remained fast and began to make water seriously. Regardless of the risk, Cook took the only course still open to him—to heave her off with the

The Endeavour River on the coast of New Holland (east coast of Australia) where the *Endeavour* put in to repair the damage caused when the ship ran on to a coral reef.

help of capstan and windlass. The move was a success and twenty-three hours after she struck the *Endeavour* was once again afloat, in deep water.

The danger was by no means over, however, as she was leaking so badly that the pumps could scarcely keep pace. For a time, it seemed as though their only hope was to try to run the ship ashore and then build from the wreckage a smaller vessel that might eventually carry them safely home. However, as an emergency measure it was decided to try to "fother" the ship; this is a technique by which a sail coated with tar and other water-proof material is drawn over a hole in the hull to seal it. One man on board, Midshipman Jonathan Monkhouse, had seen it done, and so was put in charge. It was a complete success, and in fifteen minutes the ship had been pumped dry. Tragically, Monkhouse died later on the voyage home. On 17th May, nearly a week after she struck, *Endeavour* was safely beached and repair work and general refitting were put in hand.

Not until 6th August was it possible to sail again, with only three months' provisions on board. The situation was still perilous, for the ship was surrounded by shoals as dangerous as the one that had already brought her near disaster. Eventually, however, a navigable gap in the reef was found and the *Endeavour* was once again in the open sea and able to continue northward. But the danger was still not over, for in mid-August the ship was in great peril of being dashed once again on the reef, this time from the seaward side. Just as disaster seemed inevitable a narrow gap was found, and the ship was swept through into the calmer water within. Cook's entry in his log is drily laconic: "Such are the Vicissitudes attending this kind of service and must always attend an unknown navigation: Was it not for the pleasure which naturly results to a Man from being the first discoverer ... this service would be insuportable especially in far distant parts, like this, short of

Provisions and almost every other necessary."

He goes on to remark that explorers such as he always find it hard to justify themselves to their superiors: if they are cautious they are charged with lack of perseverance, if they are too venturesome, and come to harm, they are accused of lack of prudence.

Slowly, Cook made his way north through hazardous shoals until fully 2,000 miles of the east coast of Australia had been charted. Then, at Possession Island, he formally laid claim to all this territory, as New South Wales, in the name of George III. A week's further sail took him to the south coast of New Guinea, and he was able to confirm that this territory is quite separate from Australia.

Thereafter, the voyage was uneventful in the scientific and exploratory sense. On 10th October the *Endeavour* reached Batavia, where the Dutch had started a colony more than 150 years ago; thence the long journey home round the Cape of Good Hope presented no problems save the normal hazards of the sea. Batavia offered good dockyard facilities and in a couple of months *Endeavour* was reprovisioned and made seaworthy again. Unhappily, it offered more than port facilities; it offered also dysentery and malaria, which swept through the crew. Up to the time of his arrival there Cook's close attention to hygiene and diet had prevented a single life being lost through sickness, and there had been scarcely any scurvy. At Batavia seven men died, and he left with forty men sick, of whom more than twenty died on the voyage home. Joseph Banks and Daniel Solander were among those afflicted, and were lucky to survive. The ordeal had its end, however, and on 13th July, 1771, almost exactly three years after her departure, the *Endeavour* anchored safely in the Downs, and Cook left for London to report to the Admiralty. A month later he was promoted commander.

Shelton's very accurate pendulum clock was assembled on the spot when astronomical observations were required, and to protect it from wind and weather a "portable observatory" was set up.

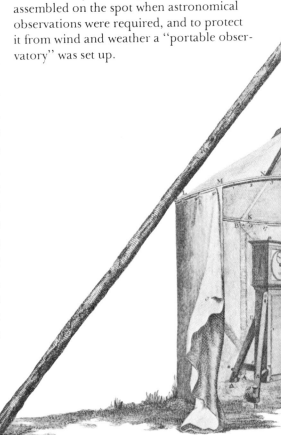

4 *The Achievements of the* Endeavour *Voyage*

The original reason for Cook's expedition was the purely scientific one of observing the transit of Venus. In this rare event, Venus passes directly between the earth and the sun, and is seen to pass slowly across the face of the sun. The essence of the observation was to time the transit from the moment at which the two disks of sun and planet just touched, to the moment at which they separated. All the instruments had been provided by the Royal Society—George III had made them a grant of £4,000—including a very accurate pendulum clock by Shelton which was put together on the spot. On the day, conditions for observation were perfect. Cook, with his usual attention to detail, arranged for an independent observation to be made by Charles Green—as he had been instructed—and also by Daniel Solander, who had brought his own telescope.

In spite of everything, however, the exercise was pretty much a failure. When combined with other observations taken at Hudson's Bay and the North Cape, long and elaborate calculations did no more than show that the distance from the earth to the sun lay between 88 and 108 million miles (the true value is approximately 93 million miles). Although the variations in James Cook's observations were criticized by the Astronomer Royal, the fault was not really his but that of the planet itself. Venus, as we now know, is surrounded by a dense cloudy atmosphere which effectively blurs the point of contact of its disk with that of the sun. That Cook realized this is clear from the note he made in his log at the time: "We very distinctly saw an Atmosphere or dusky shade round the body of the planet which very much disturbed the times of the Contacts." When the next chance came, in 1874, other observers, working under much easier conditions, found the same lack of precision. The same thing happened again in 1882, and eventually the problem had to be solved in another way.

In the matter of surveying, Cook's achievement was an extraordinary success. Often under conditions of great difficulty and danger, he surveyed no less than 5,000 miles of virtually unknown coast with a precision that in most respects has stood the test of time until the present day. In the main, as we have seen, this comprised the entire coast of New Zealand and the east coast of Australia. Thanks largely to the newly published *Nautical Almanac* he precisely pinpointed both the longitude and the latitude of all the key points he visited. He confirmed the existence of a wide strait between New Guinea and Australia.

In the eighteenth century scurvy was rife on ships making long voyages; where it did not kill it fearfully weakened its victims. Not until quite recently was it found that the disease stems from lack of a specific vitamin (vitamin C) in the diet; this vitamin is widely distributed in nature in fresh fruit and vegetables. By James Cook's time the importance of fresh food for preventing scurvy was becoming generally recognized, just from experience. As early as 1617, for example, John Woodall urged the eating of lemons and limes; half a century later (1766) John Huxham advocated the inclusion of vegetables, fruit and fruit juices in the diet of sailors. Not every captain, however, believed this, and even if they did it was advice not always easy to follow. Cook's success against scurvy was due to his never missing a chance to obtain fresh food wherever he was. He insisted, too, that the crew ate it when it was available, and was prepared to flog them if they refused. By the standards of the day he was stern rather than brutal, and there is no doubt that his crew were very much better for it.

Botanically, the expedition was a great success though, for reasons we shall see later, it was a success

An extract from *The Nautical Almanac* in its first year of publication.

A P R I L 1767.

Diſtances of ☽'s Center from ☉, and from Stars weſt of her

Days.	Stars Names.	12 Hours.	15 Hours.	18 Hours.	21 Hours.
		° ′ ″	° ′ ″	° ′ ″	° ′ ″
1		40. 59. 11	42. 34. 44	44. 9. 51	45. 44. 35
2		53. 32. 7	55. 4. 24	56. 36. 16	58. 7. 45
3		65. 39. 18	67. 8. 27	68. 37. 14	70. 5. 39
4	The Sun.	77. 22. 36	78. 48. 58	80. 15. 1	81. 40. 46
5		88. 45. 20	90. 9. 27	91. 33. 21	92. 57. 0
6		99. 52. 6	101. 14. 34	102. 36. 52	103. 59. 1
7		110. 47. 42	112. 9. 6	113. 30. 25	114. 51. 40
6	Aldebaran	50. 36. 10	52. 4. 5	53. 31. 57	54. 59. 44
7		62. 17. 43	63. 45. 10	65. 12. 34	66. 39. 57
8	Pollux.	31. 25. 48	32. 53. 11	34. 20. 40	35. 48. 12
9		43. 7. 5	44. 35. 4	46. 3. 8	47. 31. 15
10		17. 51. 57	19. 20. 36	20. 49. 26	22. 18. 27
11		29. 45. 36	31. 15. 26	32. 45. 26	34. 15. 35
12	Regulus.	41. 48. 49	43. 19. 55	44. 51. 10	46. 22. 36
13		54. 2. 11	55. 34. 36	57. 7. 12	58. 39. 59
14		66. 26. 28	68. 0. 18	69. 34. 20	71. 8. 33
15		25. 4. 34	26. 39. 23	28. 14. 26	29. 49. 44
16		37. 49. 37	39. 26. 14	41. 3. 5	42. 40. 8
17	Spica ♍	50. 48. 40	52. 26. 59	54. 5. 31	55. 44. 15
18		64. 1. 2	65. 41. 3	67. 21. 18	69. 1. 48
19		31. 37. 14	33. 19. 7	35. 1. 13	36. 43. 32
20		45. 18. 29	47. 2. 10	48. 46. 5	50. 30. 12
21	Antares.	59. 14. 6	60. 59. 31	62. 45. 11	64. 31. 2
22		73. 23. 37	75. 10. 43	76. 58. 2	78. 45. 31
23	♄ Capri-	33. 17. 26	35. 4. 38	36. 52. 4	38. 39. 45
24	corni.	47. 41. 9	49. 29. 53	51. 18. 44	53. 7. 40
25	α Aquilæ.	65. 57. 35	67. 29. 54	69. 2. 36	70. 35. 39
26		78. 24. 51	79. 59. 9	81. 33. 29	83. 7. 45

never properly exploited. Joseph Banks and Daniel Solander brought back by far the richest collection of new material ever seen in Europe—no less than 1,300 new species, distributed among more than a hundred new genera. As collectors, they had not only immense enthusiasm but exceptional knowledge and experience. They never missed a chance to acquire new specimens. Thus on the outward journey, the Viceroy of Brazil refused to let them ashore. Undismayed, they searched through greenstuff sent aboard for sheep and goats and made liberal purchases of "greens and saladding" for the table. In this way, they acquired a hundred new species.

The Swede, Daniel Solander, was ideal for the job. He had studied at Uppsala University under the great Linnaeus, who was the first to introduce systematic nomenclature into biology. This provided a system within which previously unknown species could readily be included. Briefly, Linnaeus had divided the flowering plants into some twenty classes, depending on the structure of the flowers, especially the stamens. Each plant was given a dual Latin (or sometimes Greek) name, the first showing the major class in which it was included, the second its sub-class. Other Latin adjectives might indicate finer points of classification. The Linnaean system is still the basis of botanical classification: thus we identify the common daisy as *Bellis perennis* and meadow saffron as *Colchicum autumnale*. The Latin names are not arbitrarily chosen but they describe the plant. Thus the ubiquitous Shepherd's Purse, so named because of the shape of its seed case, is almost literally translated as *Capsella bursa-pastoris*. Animals can be classified in the same way.

The system has great advantages both for naming new species and identifying old ones. Using Latin, it uniquely identifies any species, anywhere in the world, and eliminates the confusion that comes from the use of local names, attractive though these may be.

PRIMITIÆ

FLORÆ NOVÆ ZELANDIÆ

sive

CATALOGUS

PLANTARUM

in

EAHEI NO MAUWE

&

T'AVAI POENAMMOO

diebus 8 Octobris — 31 Martii

A.C. MDCCLXIX & MDCCLXX

collectarum

Above The title page of Banks and Solander's unpublished *Beginnings of a Flora of New Zealand. Above right* Sir Joseph Banks as President of the Royal Society, an office which he held for forty-one years from 1778.

Thus to the botanist Goat's Beard and John-go-to-bed-at-noon are simply and unequivocally *Tragopogon pratensis*.

Joseph Banks was nothing if not grandiose, and his idea was to publish his discoveries in a lavishly illustrated folio that would be the most splendid botanical work the world had ever seen. Unfortunately, the very magnitude of the task defeated him and formal publication was never achieved. For years the magnificent coloured illustrations languished in Banks' great house in Soho Square, London, even though in 1784 he had written, "All that is left is so little that it can be completed in two months.'' Later, it was all transferred to the British Museum (Natural History) where it still is. For scholars it has always been available, but the world has never seen it, except in parts. All the evidence is that he would have been better advised to have published the work in parts as it was completed.

Finally, the voyage provided almost the first objective accounts of the nature of the Polynesian natives. Their social and religious customs were recorded in some detail, as was the nature of their food, clothing, and houses. The scientifically inquisitive Banks devoted much attention to this, but Cook's own records show a remarkably perceptive and sympathetic understanding of the natives. It is tragic that later he was to lose his life at the hands of those whose interests he did much to protect.

"A remarkable animal found in Captain Cook's first voyage"—the kangaroo.

5 *The Voyage of* Resolution *and* Adventure

The *Endeavour* expedition had added enormously to our knowledge of the Pacific, but it still had not solved the puzzle of a great southern continent. James Cook might have done this had he chosen to come back home in a low southern latitude by way of Cape Horn, but he decided this was too hazardous so late in the year. There was still a vast area of the south Pacific which might conceal a continent. And so it was decided—barely a couple of months after Cook's return—to send out another expedition as soon as possible. It was almost inevitable that Cook should be asked to lead it for, apart from everything else, he had himself put up the idea in a postscript to his report on the *Endeavour* voyage.

A year to the day after *Endeavour* had anchored in the Channel, Cook set sail once again. This time, bearing in mind the near-disaster of the Great Barrier Reef, two vessels were sent. Both were specially bought from the same shipyard; they were Whitby ships of the *Endeavour* type, which had so fully proved their worth. One, which Cook was to command, was the *Resolution* of 462 tons; the other, the *Adventure*, was entrusted to Tobias Furneaux, one of John Byron's officers, who had sailed around the world in the *Dolphin*. The total complement was about 160 men, and some of the officers and men had served in *Endeavour*. Originally, the ships had been commissioned *Drake* and *Raleigh*, but it was later felt that these names might not be well received by Spain.

Joseph Banks and Daniel Solander were eager to venture again, and quickly collected a party of suitable assistants. Unfortunately, however, their accommodation on the *Resolution* involved so many alterations that she became, in Cook's opinion, so

top-heavy as to be unseaworthy; he had to insist that she was restored to her original state. Banks was offended, and decided not to go, although he had already spent some £5,000. It is said that his sizeable party was to have included a woman. Rather than disband it he took his expedition off to Iceland. In his place, two German naturalists were appointed—John Reinhold Forster and his son, John George Adam; they did not get on well with Cook.

With two other scientific assistants Cook was luckier. These were two astronomers, William Wales in *Resolution* and William Bayly in *Adventure*. Apart from general duties, they had two specific tasks. Firstly, they were to do position-fixing using lunars, as in *Endeavour*. Secondly, they were to make exhaustive tests of four marine chronometers which—as we have noted—could provide an easier and more precise method of calculating longitude. Of these chronometers, by far the most important was a replica of John Harrison's famous No. 4. Both men were very experienced. Wales had helped to compile the *Nautical Almanac* and had observed the transit of Venus

at Hudson's Bay; Bayly had been an assistant at Greenwich and watched the transit at the North Cape.

Cook's sailing instructions were simple and clear. He was to enter the Pacific by way of the Cape of Good Hope and then seek a mysterious Cape Circumcision which Lozier Bouvet had found on New Year's Day 1739 in latitude 54°S. Bouvet was convinced that it was part of a great southern continent. Actually, it was an isolated island which later explorers found hard to find again. If this land was not discovered, Cook was to sail south as far as he could and then turn east and circumnavigate the world in as high a latitude as possible. If the southern polar seas proved too dangerous, he was to go north and refit. As with the *Endeavour*, all members of the expedition were bound to secrecy.

Below The Ice Islands which Cook encountered on his second voyage in January 1773. The crew are cutting and collecting ice to be melted down and used for drinking.

A white bear, from a drawing by John Webber (?1750–1793), artist on the *Resolution* for Cook's third voyage.

Like others before him, Cook failed to rediscover Cape Circumcision, despite a hazardous voyage into ice-bound seas. Apart from this danger, his log illustrates other problems of navigation: not for a month after leaving the Cape did the weather allow any astronomical observation to be taken. In January, 1773, Cook gave up the search and sailed east, and on the 17th of that month crossed the Antarctic Circle, the first ship ever to do so. The *Aurora Australis*, southern equivalent of the Northern Lights (*Aurora Borealis*), was seen in these high latitudes. Bearing southward, Cook reached 67°S before ice finally stopped him: had he but known it, he was then only 75 miles from the Antarctic continent. No doubt to the relief of the crew, not all of whom shared Cook's enthusiasm for exploration, *Resolution* left those bitterly inhospitable seas and turned north for New

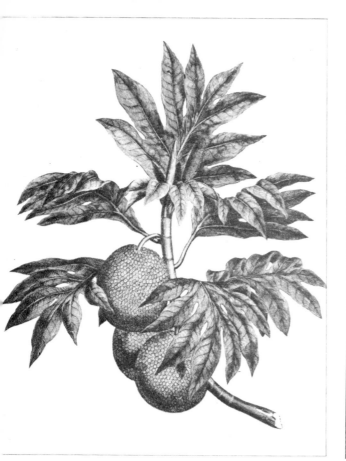

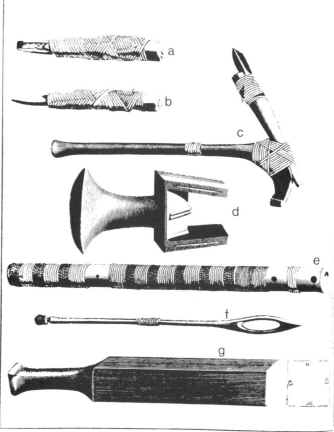

Above Bread fruit found on Tahiti in 1769.
Above right Tools of Tahiti: a & b—chisels or gouges, c—a fine cutting axe, d—an instrument to beat bread fruit into paste, e—a nasal flute, f—a thatching needle, g—an instrument for beating cloth.

Zealand to rendezvous with *Adventure*, with whom contact had been lost. This rendezvous was duly made; on 18th May. Three weeks later they were off again eastward in search of the elusive southern continent, with plans to meet in Tahiti or New Zealand if the ships were again separated. In August, they were back in Tahiti, where they received a most friendly welcome from the islanders. After only a month they were off again on a mid-Pacific cruise, in the course of which a new group of islands was discovered and named after Hervey, one of the Lords of the Admiralty: they are now known as the Cook Islands. In the course of this, contact with the *Adventure* was finally lost; she failed to join *Resolution* as agreed in New Zealand, the two ships missing each other by six days.

Alone, James Cook now set off on a crucially important cruise, one which zig-zagged across the

Left The *Resolution* and *Adventure* arrive at Tahiti in August 1773. From a painting by William Hodges (1744–97), artist on the *Resolution* for Cook's second voyage.

Below William Hodges' painting of the monuments on Easter Island, which Cook visited in March 1774. Because of a lack of resources on the island, the expedition spent only a short time there.

remaining great unexplored area of the south Pacific and finally disproved the existence of the long-sought southern continent. Or rather, we should say, disproved the existence of a hospitable continent favourable to trade and settlement. In the course of the voyage, Cook twice again crossed the Antarctic circle and turned back only when the ice made further progress impossible. The presence of sea-birds told him that there might be land beyond the ice, and he cautiously recorded: "And yet I think there must be some [land] to the South behind this ice; but if there is it can afford no better retreat . . . than the ice itself, with which it must be wholly covered."

Cook had now to decide his next move. A lesser man might have made for home, as his instructions allowed, but for Cook it was out of the question while he had a sound ship and healthy crew. There remained "room for very large islands in places wholly unexamined and many of those which were formerly discovered are but imperfectly known." He turned north and looked, without success, for the island Juan Fernandez had found in 1563 and then bore away for Easter Island with its remarkable stone statues.

Thence he set out once again for Tahiti, taking a cast around to the north, and so rediscovering the Marquesas, unvisited since Mendaña. On again to New Zealand, by way of Fiji, the New Hebrides (the Espiritu Santo of Quiros), New Caledonia, and Norfolk Island. As always, he was assiduous in his surveying and description.

On 18th September Cook was back at one of his favourite anchorages, Ship Cove in New Zealand. The message left for Tobias Furneaux was gone and he got garbled news—not clarified until much later—that one of Furneaux's boat crews had been massacred in a misunderstanding with the natives. After a stay of only three weeks, he himself finally moved towards home in mid-November 1774. He made more or less directly for Cape Horn, cutting across his earlier zig-zag

Lieutenant James Burney of the *Adventure* coming ashore in Cook Strait, New Zealand, to find the mangled remains of the ten men who had been sent ashore to gather vegetables. Burney tells us that he saw "such a shocking scene of carnage and barbarity as can never be mentioned but with horror; for the heads, hearts and lungs of several of our people were seen lying on the beach, and, at a little distance, the dogs gnawing at their entrails."

track in the same waters. In this way he still further limited the areas in which unknown islands might exist; none was in fact discovered.

In the first week of 1775 Cook sailed safely into the South Atlantic. Still a snapper up of unconsidered trifles, he set himself some further tasks before his arrival at Cape Town. The first landfall was ice-bound South Georgia, and soon afterwards the Sandwich Islands. Continuing east to the longitude of Cape Town he sailed close to, but did not sight, tiny Bouvet Island (as it is now called), the original of the long-sought Cape Circumcision, tip of a mythical southern continent. At Cape Town, a full year behind Lieutenant Furneaux, Cook heard for the first time the true story of the massacre in New Zealand.

Even now, Cook's exploring zeal was not exhausted. On the homeward voyage he made a detour to call at Fernando de Noronha, off the coast of Brazil, whose position he was anxious to chart exactly. At long last, on 30th July, 1775, he brought his ship safely to anchor at Spithead in the English Channel. He had been away from home for three years and eighteen days. He had not only circumnavigated the world again, but sailed a distance equal to three times around the earth.

In a strictly geographical sense, this second voyage was not so dramatically successful as that of *Endeavour*, with its complete survey of New Zealand and the east coast of Australia. In a negative way, however, it was no less great; the network of Cook's wake in the south Pacific left room, as he acknowledged, for more islands—perhaps quite large islands—but not for a continent. As so often, the armchair theorists were confounded by the man of action. Conjecture had been put to the test of experiment, and found wanting.

The voyage had another very important result. John Harrison's chronometer had done all that had been expected; the age-old problem of precisely

determining longitude at sea had been solved. On the
return home, after more than three years' absence, subjected to the motion of a small ship in violent seas, this
amazing watch had lost barely a minute. For this, of
course, the credit is Harrison's, but Cook played his
part: his fine feeling for instruments made sure that
the watch was properly looked after on the voyage
and, of course, his endorsement of it carried great
weight.

Above A Medallion portrait of Cook by
Josiah Wedgwood (1730–93). *Right* Portrait
of Omai, the Tahitian brought to England
by Captain Furneaux in the *Adventure*.

6 *The Fatal Third Voyage:* Resolution *and* Discovery

James Cook came home from his second voyage a celebrity. The Royal Society marked his contributions to science by electing him a Fellow in 1776 and awarding him its Copley Medal; the Navy promoted him captain; and an appointment at Greenwich Hospital ensured an adequate income. A lesser man might well have been content to relax and enjoy the fruits of his labours, but not Cook. To a friend he wrote: "A few months ago the whole southern hemisphere was hardly big enough for me and now I am going to be confined within the limits of Greenwich Hospital, which are far too small for an active mind like mine."

Events were already moving, however, to take him back to the Pacific. From Tahiti, Tobias Furneaux had brought to Britain a native named Omai, whom the government was in honour bound to take home. This alone demanded another visit to the Pacific, but Britain now had new plans for exploration there. With the final proof that there was no southern continent—at least, not in any hospitable region —thoughts were turning again to the idea of finding a new route to the Pacific around the north of America. This, it will be recalled, had been part of John Byron's orders, and success would command a magnificent reward.

As a matter of course, James Cook was consulted about the new expedition, but it was not felt fair to ask him to lead it. Cook, however, soon made it clear that, if asked, he would be more than willing to go. He thus found himself once again in command of *Resolution*, of which he had a high opinion, accompanied this time by *Discovery*, yet another Whitby-built ship. This time there were no scientists, nor was the Royal Society directly involved: such observations as were made

were entrusted to Cook and one of his lieutenants. John Harrison's chronometer, which had worked so well on the previous voyage, went with him again. Cook's crews included William Bligh, later famous in connection with the *Bounty* mutiny, and George Vancouver, who was to make a great name for himself as a Pacific explorer.

The start on 12th July, 1776, was promising. Made on the fourth anniversary of his last departure, Cook had a remarkable tribute paid to him: although a state of war existed, the rebel American colonists, France and Spain had all told their captains not to molest Cook in any way. In the case of the American colonies, a material factor, no doubt, was that Benjamin Franklin was himself a distinguished scientist.

Christmas 1776 was spent at Kerguelen's Island, discovered four years previously by the French naval officer Yves Kerguélen-Trémarec (1745–97). The view is of Christmas Harbour and shows penguins being hunted for fresh meat.

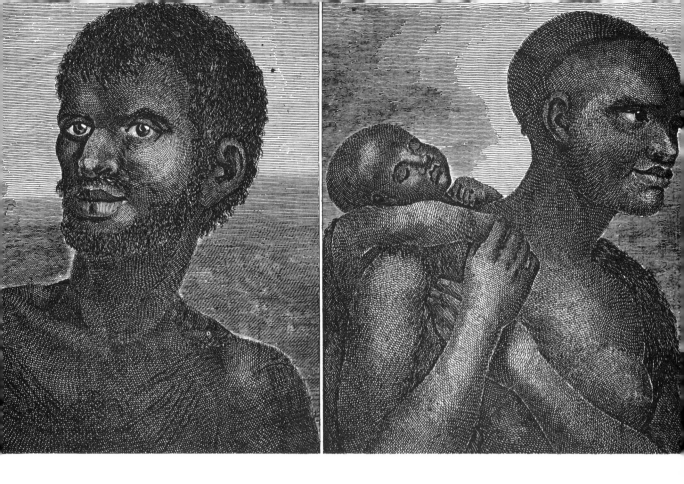

A man, woman and child of Van Diemen's Land (Tasmania), based on paintings by John Webber.

By the time Cape Town was reached, it was clear that *Resolution* was in poorer shape than Cook had believed, and another extensive overhaul was needed. However, both ships were ready to proceed on 30th November. Kerguelen's Island was visited briefly, and Christmas was spent there. On the last day of 1776, the ships set sail for Van Diemen's land, and arrived there on 26th January, 1777. Here, surprisingly, Cook made no attempt to check Furneaux's (incorrect) conclusion that it was not an island, but part of Australia. This was left to George Bass, who in 1797 sailed in an open boat through the strait that now bears his name.

By the middle of February, 1777, both ships lay safe at anchor in Queen Charlotte's Sound in New Zealand. After a fortnight's stay, they set course first for the Friendly and Society Islands, and then for

Above The inside of a house in Nootka Sound.

Opposite top A canoe of the Sandwich Islands with masked rowers. *Opposite below* Captain Cook and his officers being entertained on one of the Sandwich Islands.

Tahiti, now a familiar port of call. Omai was restored to his people, and the vessels refitted. It was time now for Cook to begin his main task. At Christmas Island—discovered on 25th December—a solar eclipse was observed. A brief visit was then paid to a wholly new group, the Sandwich Islands, where fresh provisions—for which Cook never missed a chance—were obtained. It was March before the two ships reached the coast of North America, at New Albion (now Oregon). Observing and surveying, as always, Cook worked his way steadily north—often in severe weather—until he reached the strait discovered by Vitus Bering, a Danish explorer in Russian service, in 1728. This famous strait, only fifty-six miles wide, separates Asia from America and joins the Pacific to the Arctic Ocean. On his way Cook discovered a great inlet called Nootka Sound, but failed to recognize

Sea Lions shot for fresh meat off the west coast of North America during Cook's third voyage.

Vancouver as an island. Trade, especially in furs, was established with the natives, who were quite different from those of the Pacific islands. Even Cook, used as he was to the ways of Pacific islanders, was amazed at the scale and ingenuity of their thieving.

Through Bering Strait, where contact was made with Russian traders, Cook carried on north until pack ice was reached and he was forced to turn back, giving up his search until the next summer. In the meantime he resolved to go back to the Sandwich Islands, where he found a new island, Hawaii—the largest of the group—on 30th November, 1778. This he charted, and took anchor in Kealakekua Bay. Here, to his astonishment, Cook was received not just as a friendly and distinguished visitor but as a god. Local tradition had it that a departed god would one day return on a great ship growing a forest of trees;

Cook and his party receiving a most friendly welcome on his first visit to Kealakekua Bay, Hawaii.

this description *Resolution* well fitted. As a tribute to his divinity, many provisions were given by the chiefs, though not without grumbling from the islanders, on whom the burden fell. All in all, the visit was pleasantly successful and there was mutual regret when Cook had to sail on early in February, 1779, to complete his mission.

At this point, Cook's luck changed. A few days after sailing, the *Resolution* sprung her top-mast in a gale, and repairs were essential. Reluctantly—very conscious of the inroads he had made in the islanders' supplies—Cook decided to turn back to Kealakekua Bay. As he feared, his reception this time was cool, though not actively hostile. All went well enough until on 13th February, 1779, the *Discovery*'s cutter was stolen. This was too serious a matter to treat lightly: Cook, using an old device, tried to take a native king on board as a hostage, but the islanders stopped him. A crowd gathered and a fracas broke out. In the midst of this the islanders learned that one of their number had been killed in another dispute some distance away. An attack developed, and Cook was unable to stop his marines firing; in an ugly situation he sought to re-embark his men, but he was too late. He himself was savagely attacked, and killed. At that time, his crew could not even recover his body, which was partially burned by the natives. Not for a week did passions cool enough for the pitiful remains to be recovered and decently committed to the sea.

Naturally, there were recriminations. In the inquiry that followed, particular blame was attached to John Williamson, one of Cook's lieutenants, who was said to have stayed in his boat when he might have come inshore to help. If this was true, justice was belatedly done. Some twenty years later, after the Battle of Camperdown, Williamson was cashiered for cowardice. Horatio Nelson, in his dispatches, said that he should have been hanged. The consensus of opinion, however, is that Cook's death was just the outcome of an unhappy misunderstanding, such as often happened—though rarely with such terrible consequences—when two totally different cultures came in contact with each other for the first time in history. Had Cook escaped with his life, he would probably not have taken any severe steps to exact punishment.

On Cook's death, command of the expedition fell to Charles Clerke, in command of *Discovery*; Clerke had been devoted to Cook since first sailing with him as master's mate in the *Endeavour*. John Gore, first lieutenant of *Discovery*, was appointed to command *Resolution*. Both were determined men and experienced officers, who at once resumed the main task of the expedition. On 22nd February, 1779, a week after Cook died, the voyage continued. Once again, in midsummer, Bering Strait was traversed but

Cook's return to Kealakekua was less than friendly. After a few days fighting broke out over a stolen cutter and Cook was killed trying to get his men off the beach.

ice made it impossible for the ships to go north even as far as in the previous year. Reluctantly, Clerke decided to set his course for the long voyage back to England, but once again tragedy intervened; at the age of only thirty-eight, he died of consumption, and John Gore took command. The journey home was made by way of the Kurile Islands, Japan, and Macao, thence through the Straits of Sunda to Cape Town. At the very end of it all, they had more bad luck. A storm drove them so far north that they had to make their way home around Scotland, from where dispatches were sent overland to the Admiralty. Not until 4th August, 1780, four years and three months after their departure, did the two ships finally anchor safely off the Nore.

It is hard to assess the achievements of this last voyage. Cook's death at the early age of fifty-one certainly robbed Britain of an outstanding man. No great new geographical discoveries were made. On the other hand, although the search for a passage round the north of America was a failure, it was clearly shown that ice would have made its use impracticable as a general navigational route.

The *Discovery* and the *Resolution* in the harbour of St. Peter and St. Paul (now known as Petropavlovsk), Kamchatka their first port of call on the homeward journey from Hawaii.

7 The Man and his Achievement

So far, we have given a mainly factual account of James Cook's achievements and their background, but no biography would be complete without some assessment of him as a person. This is difficult, for of Cook's private life we know little. Indeed, it is already apparent that he enjoyed rather little in the way of private life. For most of his adult years he was actually away from home at sea, in the end for very long periods. His confidant during the long absences of his Pacific voyages was his Log. Although this was an official document, destined to be read by strangers, it does sometimes reveal the man, as has already been shown by some of the extracts quoted. Apart from this, we must turn to what his contempories said about him. Fanny Burney, the novelist, found him "the most moderate, humane, and gentle circum-navigator that ever went out upon discoveries."

One quality above all that impresses one is Cook's sheer professional competence. Whatever he did, he did with a remarkable singleness of purpose, using to the full all the technical aids open to him. In naviga-tion and surveying he used the best available in-struments—including the marine chronometer for determining longitude—and whenever he could repeated each observation again and again to reduce the chance of error. He set himself, and his associates, the highest possible standard of achievement, and this was the real secret of his success.

The same determination can be seen in his fight against scurvy. He noticed that men who had plenty of fresh food, especially fruit and vegetables, did not suffer from scurvy, and went on with relentless deter-mination to see that no chance was lost to obtain fresh provisions, and to see that his crew actually ate them. The result was that, by the standards of his day, they kept remarkably fit. He summarized his ideas and experience in a paper published by the Royal Society.

Wherever he went, Cook was a keen observer of native customs, and has some claim to be recognized as a practitioner of the social sciences of ethnography and anthropology. For this, posterity must be grateful. For the native culture, the western influx into Polynesia was as destructive as that of Spain into South America. Cook's detailed accounts have a special value for their description of the Polynesian civilization before it fell under European influences. Again, however, his contribution was that of the perceptive observer rather than the trained specialist. But this was not out of line with the general course of science at that time. Men were amassing a vast amount of information which later generations would digest and classify.

Cook's election to Fellowship of the Royal Society, the oldest and most august body of its kind in the world, was, of course, an outstanding recognition of his scientific achievement, though we must remember that in the eighteenth century its membership was not so singlemindedly scientific as it is today. Cook certainly had a great regard for science, which gave him the precise instruments on which he depended for his surveys and navigation. During his limited time in England he spent much time with scientists, and his friendship with Joseph Banks survived the latter's failure to attain his ends for the second voyage.

Yet, we must be careful not to rate Cook too high as a creative scientist, as distinct from one who was ready to utilize to the full the aids that science made available to him for his professional needs. It is recorded that, once, Lieutenant James King expressed his regret to Cook that no scientists were to accompany the third expedition. Cook replied: "Curse the scientists, and all science into the bargain!" No doubt this was said in a moment of exasperation, but it contained at least a grain of truth: the somewhat rarefied

Native customs, so keenly observed by Cook, also provided good material for the ships' artists. This engraving is from John Webber's painting of a ceremonial dance in Tahiti.

84

ways of scientists must often have clashed with the severe practical problems of taking cramped vessels on long voyages across strange and hazardous oceans.

By the standards of his own day Cook was a humane man. A strict disciplinarian he was, and had to be. No voyages such as he undertook could otherwise have been made. Although he resorted from time to time to corporal punishment, he never showed the brutality which many sea captains of his day employed, and were allowed to employ. Generally speaking, he sought to get his way by persuasion rather than dictation, and this is well illustrated by a well-known story about sauerkraut (pickled cabbage). Cook had great faith in this as a preventive of scurvy, but on the *Endeavour* voyage the men refused to eat it. At Madeira he had had men flogged for refusing fresh meat, but now he tried a subtler approach. His log for 13th April, 1769, relates how he had "Sour krout" dressed everyday for the cabin table, leaving it to "the Men either to take as much as they pleased or none at all." Within a week, he had to ration the issue to the crew! He wrote with satisfaction that he never once knew this method to fail: "Such are the tempers and disposissions of Seamen in general that whatever you give them out of the Common way, altho it be ever so much for their good yet it will not go down with them . . . but the moment they see their Superiors set a Value upon it, it becomes the finest stuff in the World . . ."

Again, in contrast to the attitude of many of his predecessors and successors, Cook insisted on a tolerant attitude towards the natives. This is succinctly recorded in the instructions he drew up on the first visit to Tahiti: his men were "to endeavour by every fair means to cultivate a friendship with the natives and to treat them with all imaginable humanity." This did not rule out severe action at times, especially the taking of hostages against the return of stolen goods, but again we must recall Cook's perilous and totally

A detail from Sir Nathaniel Dance's portrait of Cook.

isolated situation. Often he was outnumbered more than ten to one by well armed natives, operating with large and skilfully manoeuvred war canoes. Even with goodwill, there was much room for misunderstanding because of totally different customs and language. To survive, Cook had to keep a moral ascendancy. We must not assume, either, that the natives were simple innocents outmanoeuvred by their sophisticated visitors. Once, when a chief had been punished for theft, he and his fellows sent their servants to steal on their behalf and had the audacity to suggest that any who were caught should be killed! A recent assessment of Cook, by an anthropologist, concludes that "so skilful was he in his relations with most islanders that among many Polynesians his name was remembered and respected for generations."

Strict though it was, the discipline to which James Cook subjected his men was less than that to which he subjected himself, and this is perhaps the heart of his character and the secret of his success. Time and again we note from his log his unfailing attention to detail, even in the face of extreme fatigue, anxiety, and hazard. He had his share of luck—except on that last fatal afternoon at Kealakekua Bay—but in the main he succeeded because he never left anything to chance. This attitude he neatly expressed in the motto to his coat of arms—*Nil intentatum reliquit* (nothing left untried).

Admiral Sir William Wharton, hydrographer of the Navy at the end of the nineteenth century and editor of the *Journal of Captain Cook's First Voyage*, wrote: "Wherever Cook went he finished his work, according to the requirements of navigation of his time. He never sighted a land but he determined its dimensions, its shape, its position, and left true guides for his successors."

Cook's grave is by a remote and lonely island: his memorial is the map of the Pacific Ocean.

Date Chart

3rd c. B.C.	Eratosthenes measures size of the earth.
1275	Marco Polo reaches China overland.
1519	Ferdinand Magellan sails from Seville to begin the first circumnavigation of the world, completed in 1522.
1555	Juan Gaetano discovers the Hawaiian group of islands.
1567	Alvaro de Mendaña discovers Solomon group of islands.
1569	Mercator publishes his World Map.
1577	Francis Drake sails from Plymouth to begin his voyage round the world.
1602	Galileo invents the pendulum.
1606	Luis de Torres discovers the Torres Strait.
1608	Telescope invented.
1615	William Schouten and Jacob Le Maire enter the Pacific Ocean by Cape Horn.
1642	Abel Tasman enters the Pacific Ocean by the Cape of Good Hope, discovers Tasmania.
1714	The Board of Longitude offers prize of £20,000 for a method of measuring longitude at sea.
1721	Jacob Roggeveen enters the Pacific Ocean.
1728	James Cook born, 27th October. Vitus Bering discovers the Bering Strait.
1731	John Hadley invents the octant.
1745	The British government offers a prize of £20,000 for the discovery of the north-west passage.
1755	Cook enlists in the Royal Navy.
1757	John Campbell invents the sextant.
1759	Cook dispatched to North America.
1762	Cook surveys Placentia Harbour, New-

	foundland; marries Elizabeth Batts.
1763	Cook appointed Marine Surveyor of the Coast of Newfoundland and Labrador.
1764	John Byron begins his world voyage.
1766	Cook observes the eclipse of the sun in Newfoundland.
1767	Samuel Wallis discovers Tahiti.
1768	Cook appointed to command the *Endeavour* expedition to the Pacific Ocean to observe the transit of Venus; sails from Plymouth 25th August.
1769	The *Endeavour* arrives at Tahiti; observation of the transit of Venus takes place on 3rd June; the coast of New Zealand surveyed.
1770	The *Endeavour* strikes the Great Barrier Reef, 11th May.
1771	The *Endeavour* returns to England, 13th July.
1772	Start of the voyage of the *Resolution* and the *Adventure*. John Harrison receives the Board of Longitude award for determining longitude at sea.
1773	Cook becomes the first man to cross the Antarctic Circle.
1775	Cook returns to Spithead in the *Resolution*, 30th July.
1776	Cook elected Fellow of the Royal Society; promoted to the rank of captain; sets sail in the *Resolution*, with the *Discovery*, on his final voyage, 12th July.
1777	Cook reaches New Zealand; discovers Christmas Island.
1778	Cook enters the Bering Strait; lands at Kealakekua Bay; is killed in a fight with natives, 14th February.
1780	The *Resolution* returns to England, 4th August.

Glossary

Anthropology The study of man and his behaviour.

Arc Part of the circumference of a circle. A whole circle is divided into 360 degrees. 1/60th of a degree is a *minute of arc*. 1/60th of a minute of an arc is a *second of an arc*.

Astrolabe An early astronomical instrument for observing the position of stars and other celestial bodies.

Back-staff A navigator's instrument for measuring positions of celestial bodies. It is so called because the observer had to stand with his back to the sun.

Bark A small sailing ship, especially a three-masted vessel square-rigged on the fore and mainmast.

Chronometer A portable timepiece of great accuracy.

Cross-staff An early navigational instrument for measuring positions of celestial bodies.

Ethnography The study of the origin and relationships of different human races.

Hydrography The study of marine surveying and chart-making.

Lead-line A weighted line for measuring the depth of water under a ship.

Log Log has two meanings: 1) A book in which daily events at sea are recorded. 2) A device for measuring a ship's speed through the water.

Meridian A giant circle on the surface of the earth, passing through the North and South Poles; the standard meridian is that which passes through Greenwich. It also means the highest point in the sky reached by the sun or a star.

Octant An instrument for measuring the altitude of the sun, stars and other celestial bodies, invented by John Hadley in 1731. It had the great advantage over its predecessors of making the observer independent of the ship's movements.

Quadrant Simplified form of *astrolabe*, used by navigators at sea.

Scurvy A disease due to vitamin deficiency and caused by prolonged lack of fresh food, especially fruit and vegetables.

Sextant Modification of the octant, invented by John Campbell in 1757. It was so called because its scale covered one sixth of a complete circle.

Picture Credits

The author and publisher wish to acknowledge their thanks to those who provided the illustrations which appear on the following pages:-
British Museum, 12, 22, 28; *Endeavour*, 3, 24, 25, 40; Mansell Collection, 61; National Maritime Museum, 16, 27 bottom, 32 top, 33 bottom, 59, 69, 80–81; National Portrait Gallery, *frontispiece*; Science Museum, 17, 20, 33 top; Victoria Picture Library, 38, 39. The remaining pictures belong to the Wayland Picture Library.

Reading List

A lot has been written about James Cook, but undoubtedly the most important single work is the massive annotated edition of his *Journals* prepared by J. C. Beaglehole for the Hakluyt Society, which itself contains an exhaustive bibliography. This work effectively supersedes the eighteenth century accounts of Cook's voyages:

J. C. Beaglehole (Ed.), *The Journals of Captain James Cook*, Vols. I–III, with a supplementary folder of charts and views. Cambridge University Press. 1955–67.

The following works are also recommended:

J. Banks, *Journal . . . During Captain Cook's First Voyage* (ed. J. D. Hooker), London. 1896.

J. C. Beaglehole, *The Discovery of New Zealand*, Wellington. 1939.

J. C. Beaglehole, *The Exploration of the Pacific*, 2nd edition. London. 1947.

J. C. Beaglehole, *Captain Cook and Captain Bligh*, Australia. 1967.

H. Carrington, *Life of Captain Cook*, London. 1939.

Endeavour, No. 100, January, 1968. Special issue to mark bicentenary of the start of the *Endeavour* voyage.

G. Finkel, *Captain James Cook, Navigator and Explorer*, London. 1969.

R. T. Gould, *Captain Cook*, London. 1939.

M. Holmes, *Captain James Cook R.N., F.R.S.: a Bibliographical Excursion*, London. 1952.

A. Kitson, *Captain James Cook*, London. 1907.

C. Lloyd, *Voyages of Captain Cook*, London. 1949.

R. and T. Rienits, *Voyages of Captain Cook*, London. 1968.

A. Sharp, *Ancient Voyagers in the Pacific*, London. 1956.

R. A. Skelton, *James Cook, Surveyor of Newfoundland*, San Francisco. 1965.

R. A. Skelton, *Captain James Cook after Two Hundred Years*, London. 1969.

M. Thiery, *Life and Voyages of Captain Cook*, 1929.

A. Villiers, *Captain Cook: the Seaman's Seaman*, London. 1967.

J. A. Williamson, *Cook and the Opening of the Pacific*, London. 1946.

G. A. Wood, *The Voyage of the Endeavour*, Melbourne. 1926.

Apart from his Log, the only major work from Cook's own pen is *A Voyage Towards the South Pole and Round the World Performed in His Majesty's Ships The Resolution and Adventure in the Years 1772, 1773, 1774 and 1775*. London. 1777.

Index

References to pictures whose captions contain information are included.

Adventure, 9, 19, 63ff, 68
Anian, Straits of, 26
Antarctic, 66, 69
Astrolabe, 17, 18, 21
Aurora Australis, 66
Australia, 25, 52, 56, 58, 71

Back-staff, 18, 19
Balboa, Vasco de (1475–1517), 10, 11
Banks, Joseph (1744–1820), 42, 43, 49, 56, 60, 61, 63, 64, 84

Bass, George (?–1812), 75
Batts, Elizabeth (1742–1835), 37
Batavia, 28, 29, 31, 32
Bayly, William (1737–1810), 64
Beginnings of a Flora of New Zealand (Banks & Solander), 61
Bering Strait, 77, 78, 80
Bering, Vitus (1681–1741), 77
Bligh, William (c. 1753–1817), 15, 74
Board of Longitude, 19

Botany Bay, 43, 53
Boudeuse, 31
Bougainville, Louis de (1729–1811), 25, 31, 32
Bounty, 15, 74
Bouvet, Lozier (1705–86), 65
Bread fruit, 67
British Museum, 42
British Museum (Natural History), 62
Burney, Fanny (1752–1840), 83

Burney, James (1750–1821), 70
Byron, John (1723–86), 29, 30, 63, 73

California, 26
Cambodia, 13
Cape Circumcision, 65, 66, 71
Cape Horn, 26, 28, 45, 50, 63, 70
Cape of Good Hope, 31, 32, 56, 65
Cape Ray, 37
Carteret, Philip (?–1796), 31
Charles I of Spain (1500–58), 14–15
Christmas Island, 77
Clerke, Charles (1741–79), 80
Colville, Charles, Lord (1770–1843), 35
Compass, 20
Cook, Hugh (died 1794), 37
Cook, James (1728–79), *frontispiece*, 8, 86
– early life, 34–5
– enlists in Royal Navy, 35
– surveys in Canada, 35, 37
– marriage, 37
– appointed to command *Endeavour*, 39
– observes transit of Venus, 47
– surveys coast of New Zealand, 49, 50
– wrecked on Great Barrier Reef, 54
– promoted Commander, 56
– appointed to command *Resolution* on her first voyage, 63
– crosses Antarctic Circle, 66, 69
– elected Fellow of the Royal Society, 73
– appointed to command *Resolution* on her second voyage, 73
– death at Kealakekua, 80
– personal qualities, 83–8
Cook, James (died 1794), 37
Cook, Nathaniel (1764–80), 37
Cook Strait, 50

Cortes, Hernando (1485–1547), 22, 23
Cross-staff, 18

Dalrymple, Alexander (1737–1808), 38, 39
Dampier, William (1652–1715), 23, 26, 31
Dance, Nathaniel (1734–1811), 8, 86
Davis, John (c. 1550–1605), 19
Discovery, 9, 73, 80, 82
Discussion of Winds (Dampier), 23
Dolphin, 30, 31, 44
Drake, Francis (c. 1540–96), 26, 27
Dutch West India Company, 29

Eagle, 35
Easter Island, 26, 29
East India Company, 28
Elcano, Juan Sebastian (?–1526), 14
Endeavour, 9, 10, 33, 40, 41ff, 53–6, 63, 64, 65, 71, 80, 87
Enisco, Francisco de (lived late 15th c.), 10
Eratosthenes (284 B.C.–192 B.C.), 12

Fernandez, Juan (1536–99), 69
Ferro, 16
Fiji, 70
Flamsteed, John (1646–1719), 16
Forster, J. G. A. (1754–94), 64
Forster, J. R. (1729–98), 64
Franklin, Benjamin (1706–90), 74
Furneaux, Tobias (1735–81), 63, 70, 71, 72, 73, 75

Gaetano, Juan (lived Mid 16th c.), 23
Galilei, Galileo (1564–1642), 19, 32
George III, 38, 43, 56
Golden Hind, 26, 27

Gore, John (lived mid 18th c.), 82
Great Barrier Reef, 10, 31, 53, 54, 63
Green, Charles (lived mid 18th c.), 41, 47, 49, 57
Greenwich, 16, 19, 73
Greenwich Hospital, 73
Grenville, 37

Hadley, John (1682–1744), 32, 33
Harrison, John (1693–1776), 19, 33, 64, 71, 74, 83
Hawaii, 78, 79, 80, 81
Hawke, Edward, 1st Baron (1705–81), 39
Hodges, William (1744–97), 68, 69
Holland, Samuel (c. 1728–1801), 37
Hudson's Bay, 29, 57, 65
Huxham, John (1692–1768), 58

Ice Islands, 64–5
Incan Empire, 24

Java, 13, 28

Kealakekua Bay, 78, 79, 80, 81
Kerguelen's Island, 74
Kerguélen-Trémarec, Yves (1745–97), 74
Kew Gardens, 43
King, James (1750–84), 84
Kubla Khan (1214–92), 13

Ladrones, islands, 29
Latitude, determination of, 16, 17, 18
Lead-line, 21
Le Maire, Jacob (1585–1616), 28
Linnaeus, Carl (1707–78), 42, 60
Log, for measuring speed at sea, 20
Longitude, determination of, 16, 19, 20, 33, 83

Magellan, Ferdinand (c. 1480–1521), 10, 11, 14, 15, 19, 21, 26, 33
Magellan, Straits of, 11, 26, 31
Mandeville, John (1300–72), 14
Maoris, 47, 48, 49
Marquesas, islands, 24, 70
Maskelyne, Nevil (1732–1811), 39, 57
Mela, Pomponius (lived around A.D. 40), 12
Mendaña, Alvaro de (1541–95), 24, 25, 32, 70
Mercator, Gerard (1512–94), 21
Mercator's projection, 21
Mercury, 35
Mercury, transit of, 49
Meridian, 16, 17, 19
Merino sheep, 43
Mexico, 24
Molucca Islands, 11, 15, 23, 26
Monkhouse, Jonathan (?–c. 1770), 55
Montcalm, Louis, Marquis de (1712–59), 32

National Maritime Museum, Greenwich, 19
Nautical Almanac, 32, 33, 58, 59, 64
New Albion (Oregon), 77
New Britain, 28
New Caledonia, 70
New Guinea, 23, 26, 28, 56, 58
New Hebrides, 25, 70
New Holland, 31, 52, 54–5
New Zealand, 28, 44, 48, 50, 51, 52, 58, 66, 67, 70, 75
Niger, 42
Nootka Sound, 77
Norfolk Island, 70
Northumberland, 35
North-West Passage, 26, 29, 73, 82

Oberea, 30
Octant, 32, 33
Omai, 72, 73, 77
Ortelius, Abraham (1527–98), 13

Palliser, Hugh (1723–96), 35, 37
Paris Observatory, 32
Parkinson, Sydney (c. 1745–71), 48–9
Pelican, 26, 27
Peru, 24
Petropavlovsk, 82
Philippines, 14, 15, 23, 29
Pitcairn Island, 15
Polo, Marco (1254–1324), 13
Possession Island, 56
Ptolemy, Claudius (c. 90—c. 168 A.D.), 12
Pulkova Observatory, 17

Quadrant, 17, 21, 46
Quiros, Pedro de (c. 1560–1614), 25, 70

Resolution, 9, 19, 63ff, 68, 73, 75, 79, 80, 82
Roggeveen, Jacob (1659–1729), 29
Royal Observatory, Greenwich, 16
Royal Society, 9, 37, 38, 39, 42, 57, 73, 83

Saavedra, Alvaro de (?–c. 1528), 23
Samoa, 29
Saunders, Charles (c. 1713–75), 35
St. Lawrence River, 32, 35
Sandwich Islands, 71, 76, 77, 78
Schouten, William (c. 1567–1625), 28
Scurvy, 14, 58, 83, 87
Seven Years War, 35
Sextant, 33
Shelton, John (1702–?), 56–7
Solander, Daniel (1736–82), 42, 43, 47, 49, 56, 57, 60, 63

Solomon Islands, 24, 31
Spitfire, 37
Stewart Island, 50
Sun, distance of, 57
Sun, eclipse of, 37, 57
Swallow, 31
Surville, Jean de (lived mid 18th c.), 25
Tahiti, 31, 44, 45, 67, 70, 73, 77, 85
Tasman, Abel (1603–c. 59), 28, 44
Tasmania, 28, 75
Teredo worm, 41
Theatrum Orbis Terrarum (Ortelius), 13
Thunderer, 37
Tierra del Fuego, 44, 45
Torres, Luis de (lived early 17th c.), 25
Trinidad, 15

Urdaneta, Andres de (lived mid 16th c.), 23

Vancouver, George (c. 1758–98), 74
Vancouver Island, 77
Van Diemen's Land (Tasmania), 28, 75
Venus, transit of, 38, 43, 44, 47, 57
Véron, Pierre (lived mid 18th c.), 32
Victoria, 14, 15
Voyage round the World (Dampier), 26

Wales, William (c. 1734–98), 64
Walker, John (lived mid 18th c.), 34
Wallis, Samuel (1728–95), 30, 31, 44, 46, 47
Webber, John (c. 1750–93), 66, 75, 85
Williamson, John (lived late 18th c.), 80
Woodall, John (c. 1556–1643), 58